Table of Contents

Foreword—By Mike Prior, Super Bowl Champion..............................6

Who Should Read This Book...9

Preface-My Journey In and Out of Being a Negative, Whiny Bitch.........11

Introduction-The Cruelness of Business and Life..........................24

Part 1-Key Principles to Keep in Mind

Chapter 1-It's a Mind Body Spirit Thing, But................................31

Chapter 2-Resilience and the "Be-Do-Have" Model........................37

Part 2: Crafting Your Unshakeable Foundation

Chapter 3: Goal Setting is Worse Than a Waste of Time...................47

Chapter 4: Alchemy of Action...55

Chapter 5: Find/Discover/Know Your Purpose..............................65

Part 3: ("T.R.A.S.H.") Your Daily Dose of Resilience

Chapter 6: My T.R.A.S.H.y Self-Discovery...................................75

Chapter 7: Tactical Vulnerability...83

Chapter 8: Radical Responsibility..96

Chapter 9: Attitude Aerobics..114

Chapter 10: Supportive Village...124

Chapter 11: Healing Humor..136

Chapter 12: Conclusion..149

Acknowledgements

To my mother and stepfather (**Janet Light** and **Harry Thompson**) who have done so much for me during a time when I truly needed it the most. Thank you both for all of your help and support. I don't know where I would be without you guys.

To **Chris, Liz, Emme, Michael Jonathan and the entire Theisen extended family** whose collective courage gave me one of the greatest gifts I've ever received, certainly the greatest experience of my life and now have become such sources of support during this challenging time for me. The lessons you've taught me and so many others were an enormous source of inspiration behind writing this book. I love and appreciate you all!

To **Mike Prior** who not only not only contributed the foreword for this book but also went from a football hero who I admired on T.V. to a good friend and mentor who's given me some really great experiences and taught me many lessons on resilience, toughness, positivity and how to be a true servant leader. Your ability to stay incredibly humble despite your accomplishments and status is truly inspiring.

To my friend **Paul Arnone** who not only has been a friend since early in high school but has been far more than just a friend. You've been a mentor, an example for how to live life with class, a "go-to" guy for so many things (including this book and the business I'm starting surrounding its subject matter. And you've been one my biggest cheerleaders and supporters on which all that I'm working.

To my friend **Pavithri Kilgore** who's been such and amazing and supportive friend and confidant with my many challenges and endeavors. Your honest, un-sugarcoated style of dealing with me has been a breath of fresh air. And your vast wisdom and life experience has made you a perfect person with which to work through so many of the challenges I've faced.

To **Ray Mills** who spent countless hours brainstorming and discussing with me many of the very ideas and the content discussed in this book. Those conversations and your encouragement played a very large part in inspiring me to write this book and start my business.

To **Lisa Dowell**, my girlfriend, who is in her own battle with stage IV cancer. Your courage, grit and determination in the face of unspeakable hardship inspires so many people, including me. And, despite your difficulties, you've remained a beacon of support, encouragement and love as I work to bring my book and business to life. I love you!

Rock Bottom

To

RESILIENT

10 STRATEGIES TO TRANSFORM YOUR MIND & BECOME UNSHAKEABLE WHEN THE SHIT HITS THE FAN

By Mark Light

Copyright © 2025 Mark E. Light

ISBN: 9798307118610

Foreword

-by **Mike Prior**, *Super Bowl XXXI Champion*

I first met Mark in 2008 through a mutual friend, where he was volunteering for an annual coaches' clinic put on by USA Football, and we also served together on the board of the Central Indiana chapter of the National Football Foundation. Mark was a regular volunteer for me in many events I held as Youth Football Commissioner for the Indianapolis Colts.

When Mark first told me he was writing a book on resilience, it made sense that he would do such a thing. I've known Mark long enough and well enough to know that he's certainly seen his share of difficulty. I've also seen how he always seems to find a way to turn the bad things in his life into something positive—for him and for others. Whether he's using his painful and dangerous bout of pancreatitis to start a foundation and then ride a bicycle across the country for a little girl suffering from the same disease (I still say he's crazy for doing that) or coming to me the very day he found out he was cancer-free after an ugly two-year battle with stage four cancer to tell me that he was going to write a book on resilience and asking me to contribute this very foreword, the dude is nothing if not resilient!

Fourteen years playing in the NFL and 20+ more years coaching football has given me the highest of highs. Like winning two straight conference championships and one Super Bowl championship with the Green Bay Packers, where I was elected by my teammates to be co-captain. It's also brought me to the lowest of lows. From being recruited by only one college to play sports out of high school, to injuries early in my NFL career, and being cut by two different teams before the Indianapolis Colts figured out I could play. Through it all,

I've learned quite a bit about football. But more importantly, I've learned a lot about life. One thing at which I think I've become "expert level" is resilience. I've had to have it my entire career. I now coach high school football players to have resilience.

Life will knock you down! No matter what you do in life—whether you're a professional athlete, coach, businessperson, or even a good friend or family member—resilience is crucial to any success you want to have, especially sustained success.

In that same discussion, when he was talking about why a book on resilience, Mark told me that for the first 30 or 40 years of his life, he was a "negative and whiny bitch." That surprised and even shocked me a little bit. I've never seen that side of Mark! What I have always seen has been a guy who is always looking to help others, whether by volunteering for the various events and clinics I hold in my role with the Colts or working with one of the various charitable organizations he seems to always be involved with.

The work he did for me would always have him working closely with other football coaches, usually from the high school ranks. This is not an easy breed of guys to impress. But Mark definitely earned their respect. One particular coach, who played at the NFL level and was now coaching at the high school level, observed Mark over three years and how he worked with prospective college athletes at a high school skills combine that I used to organize. This coach approached Mark and encouraged him to get into coaching himself, saying, "We need more guys with your calm and controlled demeanor in coaching." Mark then came to me and asked my opinion on him getting into coaching. I was all for it! I was planning to help him do so until he relocated to Texas the following spring.

Even after moving to Texas, he still kept volunteering for me anytime we happened to have an event going on while he was back in Indy visiting.

One thing I often see in my position is people who will use their connections with me and other NFL people to get tickets and other free stuff. Mark never once asked for anything for himself. He has definitely pulled a favor or two over the years, but only for things to give to someone else, usually for a charitable cause. Although, one time he did jokingly tell me that he'd like me to take him to a Packers game in Green Bay because, being seen with me at Lambeau Field, probably meant that all of his beer and food would be free!

In fall 2022, when I first heard that Mark had been diagnosed with cancer and had moved back to Indianapolis, I gave him some tickets to a Colts game, where he and a couple of his friends got to enjoy a game from field level. The following week, we met for lunch, where he thanked me for doing that for him. He looked very weak at that time, and I could tell that he wasn't feeling well. At the end of our lunch, as we were walking out, he stopped and asked me if there were any volunteer opportunities coming up where he could help me. I found myself thinking, with the way he looked, he was getting ready to go crawl into his deathbed. And yet, he's still looking for ways to help!

Then, less than two years later, we met at the same place for lunch. He looked pretty strong again. His eyes and mind seemed clear, and he told me about a whole plan that he was working on to use this setback as a way to help other people become more resilient!

I'm really not sure who or what has inspired Mark, but for him to come from where he's been to where he is now, I think a book he's written on attitude, mental toughness, and resilience is one we should all consider reading!

Author's Note: Many of the examples and stories in this book come directly from my personal struggles with the very resilience, mindset and mental toughness about which I write. Most of my adult life has been in sales of some sort. Thus, it will likely appear at times as though this is a book written for sales people, which is not <u>necessarily</u> the case. Life itself, just like a career in sales, is a minefield of difficulty and disappointment. Just being alive on earth requires the development of the skill of resilience.

Who Should Read This Book

"Hold yourself responsible for a higher standard than anybody else expects of you. Never excuse yourself. Never pity yourself. Be a hard master to yourself - and be lenient to everybody else." -Henry Ward Beecher

First, I must admit that the best time to read this book was 20 years ago. The second best time to read it is right now.

Ironically—and, yes, a bit sadly but truthfully—my experience has shown me that those who could benefit most from this book are often the ones least likely to read it. The people I imagine picking it up are already motivated individuals who are actively seeking ways to grow. They're looking to enhance their personal and professional lives, building strength in areas like character, ethics, leadership, and relationships.

When I decided to sit down and write this book, I wasn't thinking about people who already have everything figured out. Those aren't the individuals who need this kind of guidance, and frankly, they're not the ones I had in mind. This book is about transformation—it's for the person who feels stuck or dissatisfied with some critical aspect of their life. It's for the person who knows deep down that a significant change in mindset is essential to creating better outcomes, whether that's in their career, relationships, or personal growth. Most importantly, it's for someone who is ready to take that leap and implement the positive changes they know they need.

Interestingly, no matter where you see yourself right now—whether you're thriving or struggling—you're probably surrounded by people who fall on the other side of the spectrum. Take, for example, the leader of a sales team. She's likely beating her head against the wall trying to figure out how to help her underperforming team member. This individual has the potential to be a superstar but just can't seem to get out of their own way, derailed by every minor setback. That was me for much of my own sales career, constantly tripping over my own mindset.

Regardless of which camp you're in, the people who stand to gain the most from this book tend to share four key traits:

1. **Openness to self-reflection and change** – A willingness to examine habits, behaviors, and patterns and embrace opportunities for growth.
2. **A focus on long-term development** – Prioritizing sustainable growth over quick fixes or fleeting motivation.
3. **Strong character ethics** – Valuing principles like integrity, authenticity, and responsibility over shortcuts to success.
4. **A desire to make a positive impact** – Wanting to improve not just their own life but also uplift others around them.

If this sounds like you, keep reading—this journey was designed with you in mind.

Preface-My Journey Into and Out of Being a Negative, Whiny Bitch

"There is little difference in people, but that little difference makes a big difference. The little difference is attitude. The big difference is whether it is positive or negative". -W. Clement Stone

For the first 40-odd years of my life, I was probably the last person anyone would have expected to write a book about positive mindset and resilience. But here I am, writing these words less than two months after being declared *cancer-free*! In August 2022, I was diagnosed with stage four colon cancer, which had already spread to my liver by the time doctors found it. That was just over two years ago, and the journey since then has been nothing short of brutal at times.

This fight has tested me in ways I never imagined possible. Yet, as difficult as it's been, one thing has remained consistent: the role of my mental state. I don't think there's a single person in my life—friends, family, or even the medical staff—who would deny that my positive mindset has been a key factor in getting me to this point.

Resilience wasn't always my strong suit. In fact, for much of my life, I struggled to maintain a positive outlook, let alone navigate adversity with grace. But cancer forced me to dig deeper than I ever had before, to find strength and clarity I didn't know I possessed. It taught me that cultivating a resilient mindset isn't just about optimism or thinking happy thoughts; it's about making a deliberate choice every day to focus on what you *can* control, to find meaning even in the hardest moments, and to keep moving forward—even when the path seems impossible.

So, while I may not have been the obvious candidate to write this book in the past, my experiences have given me something real to share—something earned through pain, persistence, and an unwavering commitment to hope.

So, what does a guy with a historically piss-poor attitude, zero ability to "roll with the punches," and a history of being derailed by setbacks —but who somehow managed to beat cancer—have to offer to people in the business world and everyday life? Quite a bit, actually!

Stick with me—through the whole book. This isn't about lofty theories or abstract ideas; it's about survival. It's about learning, often the hard way, how to face adversity head-on and come out stronger.

The 20 Year Mind Transformation

The trajectory shift in my life didn't happen overnight. In fact, it started more than 20 years ago, so subtly that I barely noticed it at first. It was in my late 30s that I began to see positive changes in both my personal and professional life. But here's the thing—I didn't fully understand *why* things were getting better.

Because I wasn't consciously aware of what was driving this progress, the process wasn't intentional, let alone something I had mastered. I was stumbling my way forward, often blindly. And, as you might expect, there were plenty of setbacks along the way—some of them significant.

Looking back, I can see how those small, incremental shifts started to add up. But at the time, it felt like two steps forward and one step back. It wasn't a smooth or planned journey by any stretch of the imagination.

The roots of my struggles—and my deeply ingrained victim mindset—can be traced back to my early childhood. I always felt like I was a pretty smart kid, but school was a constant uphill battle, and I usually struggled badly. Then there were the "daddy issues." They started when my father became disappointed in my school performance and felt I wasn't living up to my potential in sports. That disappointment became a trigger, sending me into a downward spiral where every little challenge life threw at me felt impossible to handle.

On top of my already low self-esteem, anxiety became a constant companion, starting around age 8. The anxiety was so intense that it caused debilitating headaches nearly every day. My social skills, already shaky, stopped maturing and even regressed. My school performance, which was mediocre on its best day, started to decline even further. To cope with the mounting anxiety, I began pulling out my hair—a behavior I couldn't control. By the time junior high rolled around, I had a glaring bald patch on my head.

Any self-confidence I had left completely evaporated. I went from being one of the best athletes among my peers in grade school to one of the worst, and eventually, I quit sports altogether. Socially, I felt lost. I found it harder and harder to make and keep friends, and bullying became a near-constant experience, lasting throughout high school.

By the time I entered high school, I was desperate for any kind of escape. That's when I began experimenting with drugs and alcohol, hoping to numb the pain and anxiety that had taken over my life. What started as an attempt to cope would eventually create even more challenges down the road.

My grades went from bad to outright atrocious. In high school, it wasn't uncommon for me to turn in tests that were completely blank—or close to it—because I had paid so little attention in class and studied even less. I often didn't even have a guess to offer. Somehow, I did manage to graduate, but I'm pretty sure it was only because my teachers saw me as a lost cause and just wanted me out of their classrooms.

I graduated in the bottom 10% of my class and was genuinely shocked to discover there were people who had done even worse than I did. That revelation, far from offering any comfort, only deepened my depression. I desperately wanted to be a better person, to turn things around, but I had no idea where to start or even how to take the first step.

I felt stuck in a cycle of failure and disappointment, completely lost in the overwhelming sense that I was incapable of becoming the person I aspired to be. It wasn't just about academics—it felt like every aspect of my life was spiraling, and I couldn't find a way out. That desire to change, paired with my utter lack of direction, created a level of frustration and hopelessness that seemed impossible to escape.

I went to college, but, truthfully, I had no business being there. I had my heart set on joining the military after high school, but my dad was adamant that I go straight to college instead. At the time, Indiana State University only required a high school diploma for admission, so they accepted me, and off I went—completely directionless and with zero discipline.

I had no idea what I was doing. I changed majors as often as I changed my socks, constantly chasing something that might spark even a hint of passion or purpose. My first-semester GPA was 2.03 (out of 4.0), and believe it or not, that's the highest it ever would be. From there, it was all downhill. I spent the next two years on academic probation, and how I managed to avoid being kicked out remains a mystery to me.

My time in college was marked by poor decisions and missed opportunities. I drank like a fish, barely studied, and often skipped classes altogether. I was going through the motions without any real investment in what I was doing. After three years of floundering, accumulating roughly 60 credits but no clear path forward, I finally decided to quit.

Looking back, it's painfully clear that I wasn't ready for college—not emotionally, mentally, or academically. I lacked the structure and focus necessary to succeed, and my lack of purpose only fueled the cycle of self-sabotage. Quitting felt like a failure at the time, but it was also inevitable given the state I was in. I had hit another dead end, but it would take me years to realize that it wasn't the end of the road —it was just another detour in a much longer journey.

The Beginning of a New Way To….Underachieve

In my early 20s, I bounced between blue-collar, menial labor jobs, trying to figure out what I wanted to do with my life—*if* I ever grew up, that is. Then, almost entirely by accident, I found myself in the financial services industry at 24. Truth be told, I was hired more on the basis of being alive and available than on any particular skills I brought to the table.

That said, the man who hired me—who would go on to become my boss, friend, and mentor for several years—saw something in me. For the first time, someone outside of my family genuinely believed I had potential. That belief was something new for me, and for a while, it fueled me. I had some early success selling to family and friends, but once that well ran dry, reality hit me hard.

The "real world" of financial services was unforgiving, and I struggled badly. The only thing worse than my results was my attitude. Deep down, I believed I had no chance of succeeding in this business—or anywhere, really—and that belief seeped into everything I did. My work ethic and habits reflected the mindset of someone who had already given up. I was going through the motions, stuck in a cycle of self-doubt and poor effort, and as a result, I stayed exactly where I believed I would: nowhere.

Looking back, I realize that my mentor saw something in me that I couldn't see in myself at the time. But until I learned to see it—and believe in it—nothing was going to change. My mindset was my biggest obstacle, and it would take years before I began to understand just how much power it held over my outcomes.

After listening to a stack of motivational tapes, I stumbled across a man named Zig Ziglar, who preached about the indispensable importance of having goals. Zig's thick Mississippi drawl was captivating, and by January 1992, I decided to take his advice to heart. I set a lofty goal for myself: earning six figures by 1996. I even wrote "Six x Ninety-Six" on a postcard and taped it to the wall in front of my desk, making sure I'd see it every time I looked up. This, I thought, would be the magic bullet. After all, Zig repeated over and over, "Ya got to have them gooooooaaaaallllsssss," as though the only thing separating me from failure and top-tier success was simply setting a goal—something I'd never done in my life.

That went... well. I'm lying. It was a miserable failure, and so was I. Not only did I fail to hit my goal, but my sales steadily declined over the next four years. By 1996, I had no choice but to quit and look for another, supposedly "more secure" sales job. Unfortunately, none of those worked out either—or at least, they didn't work out for very long. I'd quit every single one as soon as the honeymoon period wore off and things got hard.

The harder things became, the more I doubled down on blaming everything but myself. The problem was never *me*. It was always the company, the boss, the lack of administrative support, the industry, the economy, the stupid customers, or even how I was raised. I was a victim of everyone and everything. In my mind, the deck was stacked against me, and I carried that victim mindset into every situation, ensuring I'd fail before I even began.

The Asshole Friend Who Shot Me Some Confidence

After a few years of bouncing from job to job—never staying in one place for more than a few months and either quitting or getting fired for poor performance—I finally found a bit of success selling pagers (yes, beepers) business-to-business. It wasn't glamorous, but for the first time in a long time, I felt like I was starting to get my feet under me.

One day, I made a sales call to a friend who, frankly, wasn't the kindest person and wasn't exactly known for dishing out compliments. Later, I heard that he had made a comment about me to someone else, and it got back to me: "Mark is wasting his talent selling pagers."

It was just one indirect nugget of encouragement, but it hit me like a bolt of lightning. This was a guy who rarely had anything nice to say about anyone, so to hear that he thought I had *talent*? It stuck with me.

That comment, paired with a bit of sustained sales success, a slowly improving work ethic, better skills, and a dash of maturity, lit a spark in me. For the first time in years, I felt like maybe, just maybe, I was capable of more.

So, I decided to go back into the world of financial services. It wasn't an easy decision, considering how poorly it had gone the first time, but I was a little older, a little wiser, and a little more prepared for the challenge. That small kernel of belief—both from someone else and from myself—became the foundation I would start to build on. It wasn't much, but it was enough to take the first step toward something better.

I wasn't exactly setting the world on fire, but I was starting to see some success. Slowly but surely, I had become a bit of a leader among my peers, earning their respect in ways that felt new and encouraging. After two years, my boss even approached me about moving into a leadership role within the company. My confidence was soaring!

One coworker even told me he could sense "an aura" around me. I'm not sure if I fully believed it, but it stuck with me—it was the kind of thing I never would have heard, let alone believed, just a few years earlier.

When the opportunity for management came up, I ultimately decided to go in a different direction. Instead of taking the leadership role, I chose to leave the company and strike out on my own as an independent financial advisor. It was a risky move, but one that felt right for me at the time.

For the first time, I felt like I was hitting my stride. The success wasn't earth-shattering, but it was steady, and it was *mine*. After years of feeling like I was treading water—or worse, sinking—I was finally starting to see some real, tangible progress. My work ethic had improved, my skills were sharper, and I was beginning to believe I had what it took to build something worthwhile.

The decision to go independent marked a turning point for me. It wasn't just about financial success; it was about owning my choices, taking responsibility for my outcomes, and proving to myself that I could do more than just survive—I could actually thrive.

Success, Setbacks and the Fight For Survival

But even that success would end up being short-lived. The events of 9/11 and the ensuing panic it created made life difficult for everyone in the financial services world, and I was no exception. Just when it felt like we were finally emerging from those market challenges, I was hit with a personal one that would change everything: I was hospitalized with pancreatitis, an incredibly painful and potentially deadly disease that would plague me intermittently for the next 13 years.

In a desperate attempt to regain my footing in the business, I began recommending a risky but highly profitable tax-saving strategy called a welfare benefit trust to my business owner clients. These programs, although completely legal and approved by my broker-dealer company's compliance department, were risky because they operated in a tax law loophole that could be closed by the IRS at any time. (For the record, I fully disclosed these risks both in writing and verbally to each client I presented them to.)

At the time, I was making a handsome living selling and implementing these programs. Business was good, and I thought I had found a way to not only stay afloat but thrive in the midst of the chaos. But then, in October 2007, while I was in the hospital dealing with a particularly life-threatening episode of pancreatitis, I received the devastating news: the IRS had indeed closed the loophole on the welfare benefit trusts that had been paying me so well.

It was a crushing blow. Not only was I battling a serious health crisis, but now, just as I was beginning to stabilize my business, everything

I'd built was threatened. It felt like life was stacking the odds against me once again, just as I had begun to gain some momentum.

Having the rug yanked out from under me with the welfare benefit trust issue, combined with nearly a year of battling serious health problems and the devastating market collapse of 2008, eventually proved to be more than I could overcome. I was forced to leave the financial services industry once again in search of "greener professional pastures." It felt like my world had crumbled, and I found myself once again adrift, completely lost, with no direction or purpose.

Things only seemed to spiral further. I ended up getting sued by one of my welfare benefit trust clients, adding another layer of stress and shame to my already crumbling situation. As if that weren't enough, in 2016, my 27-year marriage—the one thing that had felt relatively stable throughout my adult life—suddenly collapsed without warning. It was a gut-wrenching blow. Even my wife of 27 years had finally had enough of me.

It was hard to swallow, and even harder to accept. For years, I had clung to the idea that the one constant in my life could be my marriage, but now that, too, was slipping through my fingers. The weight of all these losses, one after the other, left me questioning who I was and where I was going. What was the point of trying anymore when everything seemed to be falling apart around me? But even in those dark moments, deep down, I knew that if I was ever going to rise again, I'd have to find a way to push through.

The Beginning of Real Change

Even though my world seemed mostly in shambles, groundwork had been quietly laid years before for some truly beautiful things to start happening. One of the more positive outcomes came when, along with one of my pancreas doctors, I co-founded The Pancreatitis Foundation. Our primary mission was to provide support for patients and families affected by this devastating disease, and it became a way for me to channel my struggles into something meaningful.

Around 2008, as a way to regain my fitness and strength after more than a year of battling pancreatitis, I took up cycling. What began as a way to rebuild my health quickly blossomed into a major passion of mine. Cycling became a therapeutic outlet—a way to clear my mind and feel alive again. It wasn't long before that passion evolved into a dream: riding a bicycle across the entire U.S.

Looking back, it's clear that these projects and passions were seeds planted during some of my darkest times. The Pancreatitis Foundation gave me a purpose beyond myself, and cycling gave me a sense of personal strength and accomplishment I hadn't felt in years. In the midst of my losses, I began to build something new, something that made me believe I could still find purpose and direction. Little did I know, these efforts would eventually lead to opportunities I couldn't have imagined at the time.

Up until this point in my life, I'd never been the type of person to go out of my way to help anyone unless there was something immediate in it for me. And the idea of thinking of myself as "adventurous" would have been downright ridiculous. I had never been that person. However, the process of working with people affected by the very disease that had already nearly killed me a couple of times turned out to be incredibly rewarding from the start. It gave me a sense of purpose I never knew I had, something that made the struggles I had endured feel like they had meaning.

Then, in my mid-40s, I began to realize that doing things that once seemed completely crazy—like riding a bicycle across the U.S.—was no longer just a passing passion. It was becoming something of an obsession. The more I immersed myself in the idea, the more it consumed me, and in the best way possible. It wasn't just about the challenge of it anymore; it became a symbol of everything I had overcome and a way to test my limits.

As I look back, it's fascinating how these seemingly random interests and pursuits began to reshape my life. What started out as a way to find meaning and purpose in the face of illness and hardship eventually became a driving force in my life. The crazy dream of cycling across the country wasn't just a goal—it was a manifestation of the growth and resilience that had come from years of struggle. And it gave me the courage to keep pushing forward.

Then, in the fall of 2016, I finally lived out my dream of riding a bicycle across the USA. As good fortune would have it, this journey turned into something far more meaningful than I could have imagined. It became a fundraising mission for a 3-year-old girl from Noblesville, IN, who was suffering from a childhood form of pancreatitis and urgently needed a life-saving surgery. What started as a personal goal quickly transformed into a cause far greater than myself.

This journey would go on to profoundly alter the course of my life. Along the way, I encountered countless stories, people, and experiences that shaped my perspective and deepened my understanding of resilience, purpose, and the power of giving. Many of these encounters led to valuable lessons that I'll be sharing throughout this book. What began as a physical challenge became a transformative journey, not just for the girl I was helping, but for me as well. The lessons I learned during those long miles are the same ones I carry with me today, and I hope they'll resonate with you, too.

The journey would take me across the vast state of Texas, a place that would later become my home the following year. It was in San Antonio, Texas, where I would receive the life-altering diagnosis of colon cancer in August 2022. Faced with the overwhelming reality of my condition, I knew I needed to be closer to my support network. So, I made the difficult decision to move back to Indiana, where I had a much stronger base of family and friends who could help support me through this next chapter of my life.

But the most groundbreaking realization of all was the discovery of the massive village of friends and family who had been supporting me every step of the way. This made me realize that, despite all my lifelong miscues, missteps, and outright stupidity, I must have done a few things right along the way. It prompted a lot of soul-searching. I came to understand that my entire life had somehow prepared and equipped me for this diagnosis. Instead of asking myself, "Why me?" I found myself genuinely saying, "Thank God, me!"

Life had prepared me for this incredibly difficult path, and, for the first time in a long time, I truly felt ready.

In the coming chapters, I'll walk you through exactly what I got right in my life so that you can intentionally emulate this process. My hope is that, through my experiences, you'll find practical ways to build your own resilience and strength—just as I've learned to do over the years.

Introduction-The Cruelness of Business and Life

"(When doing something scary or difficult or painful, or you find yourself in a difficult situation)…you've got to take great pleasure in the fact that nobody wants to be where the fuck you're at right now" -David Goggins

In January 1996, I was a young, struggling financial advisor, consumed by self-doubt and desperately searching for every crumb of business I could get my hands on. In my frustration, I made the decision to go against the advice and wishes of my manager and started a cold calling campaign—something that was well outside my comfort zone. (And yes, it's true, I actually worked for a sales manager who believed cold calling was "too negative.") The thing is, despite the reluctance and skepticism, it was working when nothing else was.

At that point, I had little to lose, and cold calling became my last-ditch effort to make any real progress. What began as a desperate measure soon became a crucial part of my journey, showing me the power of pushing past my comfort zone and trying things I had never considered before. Sometimes, the very thing we resist the most turns out to be exactly what we need.

Well, soon enough, my efforts resulted in a meeting with a man named Burley. Burley was an elderly gentleman who, despite never having heard of me before, invited me to his home to discuss some financial concerns he had. Upon my arrival, he almost immediately told me that he had $60,000 sitting idle in his checking account and felt it should be put to work for him. This was a big deal, as that $60,000 represented a very significant account for me at that stage in my career, should I be fortunate enough to "win" his business.

After a lengthy Q&A to understand his needs, risk tolerance, and so on, I told him I would go back to the office, prepare a proposal, and return in a few days to deliver it.

Upon my return, I delivered the proposal to Burley. As he looked it over, he said, "You really seem to know what you're talking about," and reached for his checkbook. He proceeded to write a check for that $60,000 to place into an investment account. As he wrote the check, I noticed his hands began to shake. In that moment, my immediate thought was, "I better get this check, get out of here, and deposit it before he changes his mind!"

STUPID MOVE BY ME!

In hindsight, I realize that I missed a crucial opportunity to pause, to acknowledge the gravity of the moment, and to handle it with more care. But in that instant, driven by my urgency and desperation, I made the classic mistake of rushing through what should have been a more thoughtful and professional process.

I went back to the office with the check, deposited it into his investment account and was paid a pretty handsome commission by the end of that week. Early the next week, after I had already received the payment, I found out that Burley had stopped payment on the check as soon as I walked out of his house. I had to give back the much-needed commission. To say I was devastated would be a massive understatement! I was absolutely crushed. All I could do that day was leave the office, go home, lay in bed, and cry. I was so gutted by this, I could barely summon the energy to prospect for weeks. The weight of the situation left me paralyzed, questioning everything— from my abilities to my judgment. It felt like a punch to the gut, and it took everything I had just to get through the days following.

Sales and entrepreneurship are filled with setbacks, uncertainty, failure, pain, rejection, and the discomfort of prospecting. That's the problem at work. But the truth is, life itself can be difficult, whether at home or in any walk of life—not just in sales. We all face challenges, big and small, that test our patience, resilience, and drive. And it's not just the professional struggles that weigh us down; the personal battles we fight can often be just as relentless. Whether it's managing relationships, health issues, or simply staying afloat during tough times, everyone deals with their own kind of hardship. But here's the thing—each of us has the power to decide how we respond to it. The strength we build in the face of adversity shapes us in ways we never see coming. It's not about avoiding the discomfort, but learning how to move through it.

Now, imagine you're in a leadership position where low resilience is the norm. What does that lack of resilience, poor mindset, and absence of mental toughness do to your culture? I had a boss once who would often confide in me, complaining that his entire sales team—my coworkers—was lazy. The team was made up mostly of young, inexperienced men and women who were new to sales. One day, I asked him, "What if that tree," pointing out the window of his office, "suddenly sprouted and began growing $100 bills? These people, who you're calling lazy, would probably show a work ethic that would blow your mind." I was trying to nudge him to see that these individuals needed him to step up and actually lead them. What often appears, on the surface, as poor work ethic or other character flaws is frequently nothing more than fear and self-protection at play. People aren't born with a lack of resilience; it's often cultivated by the environment they're in. And as a leader, it's your job to help shift that environment, to show them the way forward, and to foster the mental toughness they need to thrive.

And if you bring a top-tier performer into a low-resilience culture, it usually goes poorly. In very few cases does the top performer manage to turn the culture around. More often than not, the toxic environment poisons the mind of the top performer, or they simply remove themselves from it entirely. (Ever been inexplicably ghosted by someone you held in high regard? Do the uncomfortable math.)

In order to maximize potential and minimize problems in any situation, having a resilient default setting within yourself is not just important—it's crucial! Without it, no matter how talented you are, you'll struggle to navigate the inevitable challenges life throws at you. Resilience isn't just a nice-to-have; it's the foundation that enables you to thrive, not just survive. Whether you're leading a team, managing personal challenges, or building something from the ground up, your ability to stay grounded, focused, and positive in the face of adversity is what will ultimately determine your success.

Resilience, a positive mindset, and mental toughness are not about simply "hunkering down" and trying to get through tough times. True resilience is about using adversity as a catalyst for growth and improvement! What I've learned through my own experiences is that it actually takes less effort to be truly resilient—by my definition of resilience, which we'll dive into in Chapter 1—than it does to quit, give up, or avoid problems altogether.

One way you can self-test whether you're resilient is to look at how you react internally when faced with unexpected difficulty. If, at least a small part of you, actually feels a sense of relief or even happiness in facing the challenge (because you know you can handle anything, and that mindset sets you apart in a very powerful way from most others), then you've developed a strong resilience muscle.

David Goggins, a former Navy SEAL turned author and motivational speaker, summed it up perfectly when he said: "(When doing something scary, difficult, or painful, or when you find yourself in a tough situation)... you've got to take great pleasure in the fact that nobody wants to be where the fuck you're at right now." Think about that for a second. Do you really believe that someone with that mindset isn't mentally ready for whatever comes their way?

On August 11, 2022, I was diagnosed with stage 4 colon cancer, a diagnosis that had already seen the cancer spread to my liver, and a couple of months later, to my lymph nodes. That diagnosis, while devastating and life-altering, turned out to be one of the best things to ever happen to me, and for far more reasons than I can possibly list.

I realized shortly after the diagnosis that, somehow, I had transformed into a completely different person. My prognosis seemed bleak, but I knew without a doubt that, even though I might not survive this, **I could deal with anything** that came my way. The "negative, whiny bitch" I'd once described to Mike Prior was officially gone—replaced by someone who was now seen by everyone as having one of the most powerful mindsets imaginable for what I was facing. And let me be clear, there's nothing fake about this newfound mindset. In fact, when I took the EQi and HRG assessments—tools designed to measure emotional intelligence, resilience, and hardiness—I scored incredibly high on both.

But the question is, how did I make that leap? That *transformation*?

I took a very deep, introspective look back at my life and realized there were things I had been doing for much of it, particularly when it came to building my Supportive Village around me. Then, in more recent years, I started a mostly unintentional journey of completely rewiring my own mind. So, it's not that I came up with these 10 strategies by any means. It's that I stumbled upon them, almost by accident. I discovered that, in my case, I had been unknowingly following this "program" or at least an inconsistent version of it, for many years.

It took me far too long to become truly resilient because I was doing it by accident. My journey with resilience was filled with ups and downs —many more downs than I care to admit. I struggled and fell backward a lot, simply because I had the formula within me but was neither aware of it nor intentional about using it.

The point of this book is to shorten the curve for **you**. The stories and anecdotes that I used to illustrate the points in this book are mostly a mix from my business and personal life. However, they're all relatable to literally any and every aspect of life! No matter what you do for a living, whether it be sales, business, teaching, healthcare, technical, or trades….even (ESPECIALLY?) Athletics, or if you find yourself facing a major personal or health-related crisis, having resilience, mental toughness and a positive mindset is going to make you better, more effective and more productive….and the journey is just a lot more enjoyable when you know for a fact that **YOU CAN DEAL WITH ANYTHING!!**

PART 1 Key Principles to Keep in Mind

Chapter 1: It's a Mind Body Spirit Thing, But…

"A Problem Well Understood Is A Problem Half Solved" -Rener Gracie

In late May 2012, I embarked on what would turn out to be the most life-changing experience I had ever had up to that point—the mission was to hike rim to rim at the Grand Canyon. Now, up until that moment, I had never been a Boy Scout, never considered myself "adventurous," and had never even gone on a real hike in my life. But my friend, Tim Roberts (a.k.a. "The Judge"), an avid and seasoned outdoorsman who had accomplished this feat three times before, encouraged me to take on this adventure. He also mentored me on how to prepare for it, and along with his wife, Pam, joined me on the journey. I would have NEVER taken on something like this without him there to guide me—at least not at that point in my life.

When I arrived at Grand Canyon National Park to meet Tim and Pam, I wasn't entirely sure what to expect. What I did know was that, after months of very specialized workouts, my body was likely ready. I also felt that Tim had mentally prepared me for what I was about to face. Hiking the Grand Canyon is no joke! For the uninitiated, we began our trek on the South Rim at 5 a.m., with an elevation of around 7,500 feet and temperatures in the mid-30s. By noon, after crossing the Colorado River, we had descended 5,000 feet, and the temperature had soared to over 100 degrees.

Surprisingly, the hike down into the canyon, which might seem like it would be easier than the climb up and out, was actually more grueling. It beats you up physically. Toenails are lost, and your knees and back take a serious beating with each hour of tapping down the rocky trail, all while carrying 30–40 pounds of food, water, and gear on your back. It's a 21-mile trek that we chose to complete over three days. On top of the sheer physical exhaustion, the canyon has a way of breaking you down mentally, leaving you with nothing but your character. And, in my experience, you either come to terms with the person you truly are, or you don't. I found that I liked myself more than I had realized.

But perhaps the most remarkable thing about the Grand Canyon is its breathtaking, almost otherworldly beauty—a level of magnificence that literally boggles the mind!

For me, I passed both the physical and mental tests thrown at me by this incredible hole in the ground—but I was well-prepared for that. What I didn't expect, however, was what the Grand Canyon revealed to me from a spiritual standpoint. It's hard to put into words, but when I completed that hike, it felt as though I had spent three days in the direct presence of God. I had never experienced anything so powerful. The whole journey changed me as a person. In fact, I think it revealed a version of me that I had never known existed. And for the first time, I felt almost invincible.

And, to make a long story short, things on this hike did not go as planned. We ran into unexpected trouble, and at times, it became downright scary. But that only added to—and enriched—the entire experience!

When your mind, body, and spirit are all firing on all cylinders, problems simply don't derail you as easily.

To be truly effective, resilience becomes a "mind-body-spirit" equation. While this book focuses primarily on the "mind" portion of that equation, we're taking a moment in this chapter to pay homage and stress the importance of nurturing the body and spirit, emphasizing that they are just as crucial to the overall equation as the mind is.

Treat Your Body As If You Like the Person Who Owns It

You have one body—treat it like you mean it! To be truly resilient, you must have a fit mind. And it's nearly impossible to have a fit mind without also having a fit body.

So let's talk about exercise for a moment—or as we Apple Watch users like to say, "closing those rings." One thing I've consistently gotten right in my life is physical fitness. I'm also someone who's faced numerous serious, life-threatening health issues. I can't tell you how many doctors and nurses have told me over the years how fortunate I am to have remained so fit, and how my fitness level has likely saved me from what could've taken down others my age. Friends often ask me for advice on getting fit. The good news? You don't need to be a fitness fanatic, you just need to avoid being sedentary.

At its core, all you really need to do, at least to start, is find something you enjoy that involves physical activity and that you could do every day from where you are (gardening, for example, is a great choice). If you're new to exercise or just dread it, start smaller than you think you should. I used to advise people to start by simply getting to the gym. Don't even worry about going inside at first. Just sit in your car, listen to the radio for 15 minutes, and then go home. After a week or so, once you've built the habit of consistency, start going inside. I know it sounds strange, but we'll dive into why this actually works in Chapter 3. You don't need to be obsessed; you just need consistency.

And you've got to eat your veggies! I'm a living testament to the dangers of not paying attention to what you consume. Partly fueled by the compliments and encouragement I was receiving from medical professionals about my fitness—and how much I seemed to skate by because of it—I completely neglected my diet. That mistake nearly cost me my life.

As I write this, however, I'm in the process of completely overhauling what I put into my body. I'll spare you the details of my journey, but just know that I'm learning and working through a process that's very much like what we'll discuss in Chapter 3.

One tip on diet that I'll share is actually a book recommendation. Shortly after my cancer diagnosis, my health insurance guy, Tony Nefouse, told me about the book *How Not to Die* by Dr. Michael Greger. Talk about an attention-grabbing title for someone who just received a cancer diagnosis! The book is a highly detailed "manual" on how lifestyle and diet can drastically impact your health. Tony mentioned that he had seen many clients with poor health situations completely turn things around after reading and implementing the advice in this book. So, I bought it and read it.

The shortest way I can put it is, I'm no dietician, but this book is brilliant, well-thought-out, and backed by a *shit-ton* of science. I tried implementing its principles while going through chemotherapy, but I was forced to abandon it. Being plant-based, I simply couldn't get the necessary volume of food on board to maintain weight because of my chemo treatments, and my weight was dropping. My oncologist recommended that it was far more important to maintain my weight during chemotherapy than to focus on eating healthy.

Now that I'm off chemotherapy (for now), I'm starting to gravitate back toward a more plant-based diet.

Bottom line: *"Garbage in, garbage out. Good stuff in, it goes to your head."*

Nourish the Soul as Well

Kurt Warner is a former NFL quarterback, now in the Hall of Fame. But his career almost didn't even happen. And, when it did, things did not go smoothly for him. Warner's journey from being an undrafted player working in a grocery store to a Super Bowl MVP is often attributed to his deep faith and spiritual resilience. His persistence and reliance on faith helped him overcome numerous setbacks, including being cut from the Green Bay Packers and enduring a period of financial struggle. His spiritual foundation gave him the strength to persevere, eventually leading him to success with the St. Louis Rams and Arizona Cardinals, all while maintaining humility and a strong commitment to his faith.

For many, spirituality is about faith, their church and/or their religion. That's simply never been my thing, and God knows I've tried to make it so. However, if church and religion are your thing, I 100% respect that. Spirituality is a highly personal thing. for me, a bicycle seat is a kin to a church pew. And for me, hiking down to the bottom of the Grand Canyon is like entering a sanctuary, same with riding a bicycle through the mountains or even just an open deserted country road at dawn. And not to get ahead of myself (Chapter 9), but a simple act of kindness or gratitude is like prayer to me. I've actually had people imply that I'm going to hell for my source of spiritual nourishment and that it doesn't come from organized religion for me. Let's hope that doesn't happen here.

On the other side, I have little doubt that there are people who likely poo poo spirituality altogether. I really don't think that's correct either and science agrees with me: The National Institute of Health, in a 2023 article "The Relationship Between Spirituality and Resilience and Well-being: a Study of 529 Care Leavers from 11 Nations" it was cited that "Spirituality seems to serve as a factor that guides people through life challenges and functions as a pathway to resilience and maintaining well-being" (https://www.ncbi.nlm.nih.gov/pmc/articles/PMC9918825/

Overall point here is, to become truly resilient, nourish and exercise your spirit and body as much as you do your mind.

Duh!

Chapter 2: Resilience and the "Be-Do-Have" Model

"Everyone has a plan until they get punched in the face" -Mike Tyson

On September 7, 2022, just less than a month after my cancer diagnosis, I posted to my Facebook page this open letter to cancer:

"Dear Cancer,
I'm writing to let you know that, even though we will soon be opponents in "the octagon of life", I'm actually NOT hating you the way you hope that I will. While, it's my intent to kick your ass, I completely respect the fact that you're here to kick MY ass as well. You're a formidable opponent and you've got experience (and a head start) on your side. You've been KILLING people like me for centuries!! You've evolved and reinvented your game constantly since you were first born. Hell, I'll admit…even though I'm ready for you….and I've got skills, experience and moves of my own, there's a decent chance you could beat ME just like you've put down so many others before me. No matter the outcome, you and I will never be friends, but I RESPECT YOU for that much at least!! And let's face it, you've even got a "4 stage head start on me, you clever little fuck!

So, ultimately, as we get ready to "touch gloves" in the coming days, I just want you to think about this: No matter who beats who in this fight, you ARE and always will be MY BITCH!! Your game is built almost entirely upon getting me to fear and hate you AND your little corner-mate in the black outfit (his name is Death). I can already see that you both are a liiiiiittle psyched out by the fact that I'm genuinely not the least bit intimidated by your dirty little tactics…..and besides, I feel like Rocky because the crowd is already chanting MY name and we haven't even gotten in the ring yet! I'm feed off THEIR support

even more than you think! (But, you're used to being the "sexy villain"). So, In a very real way, even though the first punches haven't even been thrown yet, I've already beaten you…..even if you knock me out. That HAS to be fucking with your mind just a little. I know it would mine.
Anyway, I wish you luck.
LET'S GET IT ON!!
Sincerely,
Mark"

And here's the thing—I meant every last word of it & believed it down to the very core of my existence. You see, before cancer ever even entered the picture, I had already spent years battling severe health problems like necrotizing pancreatitis and bacterial meningitis. Both were excruciatingly painful. Both nearly killed me. I'd stared down the barrel of the proverbial "sick" and "death" guns so many times before—and somehow managed to overcome every single one of them—that cancer didn't intimidate me. Not one bit.

I knew I was in for a fight, and I was so damn ready for it that I almost felt sorry for the cancer! Yes, I was the underdog, and I knew the odds weren't in my favor. But I also knew one thing for certain: ***I could deal with anything***.

Be-Do-Have—An Updated Version of It

The "Be-Do-Have" model isn't a groundbreaking concept, but it's one that packs a punch. For those unfamiliar, it breaks down like this: to HAVE something, you first need to DO something (probably a lot of somethings, if we're being honest). But before you can truly *do* those things effectively, you've got to BEcome something. Simple enough, right?

Most people intuitively get this. But here's the kicker—most people stop there. They miss a crucial layer. I believe there's an often-overlooked lowercase "do" that has to sneak out in front of the big, bold "BE." That little "do" is where the spark ignites, the momentum starts to build, and the *transformation* begins.

At the start of my cancer battle, I knew I wanted one thing: to HAVE my health back. To get there, I understood that what I needed to DO was treat this as the fight for my life that it truly was. But here's the thing—facing a high-stakes fight like this meant I had to BE a fighter, and I wasn't naturally wired that way.

What transformed me—what unintentionally *forced* me to BEcome the fighter I needed to be—was the gauntlet of serious health challenges I had already faced years before. Those experiences were my "do." They shaped my "BE," which, in turn, empowered me to DO what was necessary to fight cancer and, ultimately, to HAVE the chance to reclaim my health.

Spoiler alert: this same principle will resurface with a fresh perspective in Chapter 7. Stay tuned!

In August 2016, just three weeks before I set off on my cross-country bicycle journey, I made a call to a friend to ask for a small favor. That friend was Bill Brooks—a retired NFL wide receiver who had an impressive career with the Indianapolis Colts, Buffalo Bills, and Washington Redskins during the late 1980s and 1990s. Bill and I had gotten to know each other while serving on a non-profit board together, and I knew him to be as kind and humble off the field as he was talented on it.

One morning, I picked up the phone and asked if he'd be willing to record a short video promoting my cross-country journey to help with my fundraising efforts. Without hesitation, Bill agreed.

I replied, "Great! I'll meet you this afternoon, give you the rundown on what this whole thing is about and why I'm doing it, we'll shoot the video, and I'll be out of your hair in five minutes."

That afternoon, when we met, I explained, "I'm riding my bike across the United States to raise money for a little girl who's battling pancreatitis—a disease that nearly killed me. She needs a surgery to help save her life."

Bill looked at me for a long moment, then asked, "By 'bike,' you mean 'motorcycle,' right?"

I shook my head and mimicked pedaling with my hands.

He blinked, clearly trying to process this, then said, "OK, but you'll have a vehicle following you the whole way, won't you?"

"Nope," I replied, grinning. "Just me, my bike, and all my camping gear."

Bill stared at me, his eyes full of genuine concern, and finally said, "Mark, I don't think this is a very good idea!" He said it in a way that made it sound like I'd just dreamed up the whole plan that morning on a whim.

I couldn't help but laugh. "Bill," I said, "you made your living going up against guys who were literally trying to separate your head from your neck—and they were more than capable of doing it. The fact that *you* think I'm crazy tells me I'm doing exactly what I should be doing!"

Looking back, it wasn't until about a year after I successfully completed that mission that I realized something: a lot of people had been watching it unfold on Facebook, waiting for what they were certain would be an inevitable "flame out." In the months and years leading up to the journey, when I told people about my dream to ride across the country, many couldn't even wrap their minds around the idea. They questioned whether it was even possible, often with raised eyebrows or polite disbelief.

And then, in the summer before the ride, when I was heavily promoting it and making my final preparations, plenty of others tried their damndest to "talk sense into me." They thought they could convince me to abandon what they saw as a reckless, unrealistic, and borderline insane plan.

See, what Bill and all the other "pragmatic" people couldn't have known was the years of preparation I had poured into learning and lowercase "do"ing to BEcome a cross-country cyclist.

It wasn't just about logging miles—though there were plenty of those. I deliberately put myself into situations that might've seemed ridiculous to anyone watching but were critical for preparing me to face whatever challenges might arise, hundreds or even thousands of miles from the comfort of home. For example, I read that getting caught in a thunderstorm for the first time on a bike shouldn't happen when you're out in the middle of nowhere. So, I waited for a storm— lightning, thunder, the whole nine yards—hopped on my bike, and rode a 25-mile trek.

I taught myself everything I could about basic bike maintenance and repair, knowing I couldn't afford to be helpless in the middle of nowhere. I studied gear meticulously, figuring out what was truly essential versus what was just "nice to have." I left no stone unturned, making sure I was as prepared as humanly possible for whatever the road might throw at me.

When the ride finally started, I knew it would be a 3,000-mile journey, and I hoped to enjoy at least 2,000 of those miles. The other 1,000? I figured I'd just have to gut it out. And, sure enough, unexpected problems cropped up along the way. I dealt with route issues, mechanical breakdowns on the bike, unpredictable weather, and even my own body betraying me at one point.

But all the preparation I'd done—getting my mind and body right, learning the skills I'd need—had firmly cemented the "do" in front of the "Be-Do-Have" approach I'd applied to this adventure. Because of that, instead of enjoying only 2,000 miles as I'd hoped, I savored every single one of them. Even when things went sideways, I found joy in the experience. Why? Because I knew—down to my core—that no matter what the road threw at me, **I COULD DEAL WITH ANYTHING**!

As a rookie financial advisor, my imposter syndrome held me back from *doing* what I knew I needed to do. It wasn't until I gained a much deeper understanding of my craft, became fully credentialed, and honed my soft skills—like sales and communication—that I earned the confidence to *be* the professional I needed to be. That shift allowed me to consistently *do* what was necessary to *have* the success that eventually made me an "Excelsior Producer" for my broker-dealer/general agency.

Tools like Neuro-Linguistic Programming (NLP) and Cognitive Behavioral Therapy (CBT)—both well-established and backed by psychological science—further validate the BE-DO-HAVE model and offer practical, actionable guidance on how to apply it in real life.

Neuro-Linguistic Programming (NLP) is a psychological approach that explores the connection between neurological processes (neuro), language (linguistic), and behavioral patterns learned through experience (programming). It focuses on understanding how individuals perceive and interpret their world, and how this influences their communication, emotions, and actions. At its core, NLP aims to empower individuals to reprogram their thoughts and behaviors to achieve specific outcomes. It involves techniques like reframing negative beliefs, modeling successful behaviors, and using positive language patterns to foster confidence and growth. By improving self-awareness and interpersonal skills, NLP helps people overcome limiting beliefs, develop a more positive mindset, and unlock their potential to thrive in personal and professional settings.

Cognitive Behavioral Therapy (CBT) is a widely practiced, evidence-based psychological approach that focuses on identifying and changing negative thought patterns and behaviors. It is based on the premise that our thoughts, emotions, and behaviors are interconnected, and by addressing unhelpful or distorted thinking, we can positively influence our feelings and actions.CBT helps individuals recognize automatic negative thoughts, challenge their validity, and replace them with more balanced, constructive perspectives. It also emphasizes practical strategies like problem-solving, stress management, and goal-setting to improve overall well-being.Through structured techniques, CBT empowers people to break cycles of negativity, manage challenges like anxiety, depression, and stress, and cultivate a healthier, more resilient mindset. Its practical, goal-oriented approach makes it a powerful tool for fostering long-term personal growth and mental wellness.

I've always believed that both NLP and CBT are incredibly sound tools, but they're incomplete. I'm skeptical that a negative mind can truly reverse itself for the long haul without some form of external influence or intervention. These techniques often work almost like magic, but without additional input or reinforcement, their impact can be short-lived.

That said, if you're aiming for anything worthwhile in life, the BE-DO-HAVE model remains the ultimate guide—the blueprint, the game. I just think it benefits from a little enhancement, a touch of icing on the cake to make it truly stick.

Coaching Great Agrees With Me

In Rick Pitino's book *Success is a Choice*, he articulates the very principle I'm discussing right from the start. The first 10 pages, nestled between the Introduction and Chapter 1, contain a section called "Deserving Victory." In this section, Pitino emphasizes how hard his teams practice and prepare, and how that effort pays off in close, competitive games when everyone is exhausted and running on fumes. When the difference between winning and losing is "as thin as an eggshell," it's during those times that all the blood, sweat, and tears of practice truly make a difference. As Pitino puts it, those are the moments when his players look at one another and feel that they deserve the victory because they've worked harder than the other team. He also notes that, in reality, they have no idea how hard the other team has worked, but that's irrelevant. Who outworked whom is not the point. The point is that his teams genuinely believe they've worked harder and therefore deserve the victory more. This hard-earned belief in themselves is what gives them that extra bit of energy, the added fight, and the confidence in each other that often pushes them over the top toward victory. It's their edge. And they earned it!

Pitino's book is over 270 pages long, filled with a lot of good stuff, and I highly recommend it. However, the key point was made in those first 10 pages. Had Pitino left that one element out or simply glossed over it, the entire book would, in my opinion, lose its impact. This part is the foundation.

Life offers no guarantees. Rick Pitino's teams sometimes lose to teams that are mentally stronger than they are. And no matter how prepared you are for anything, life will still knock you flat on your ass. So, it's ultimately about creating that solid foundation of deserving success. In order to get the "BE-DO-HAVE" ball rolling and keep it rolling long-term, you must give your brain substantial evidence that the "BE" is real. You can try to bullshit yourself, but not for long. Your mind will eventually figure you out.

Frankly, the purpose of this entire book is to provide you with the tools to place that lowercase "do" out front, giving you the late-game edge of deserving success and knowing that **YOU CAN DEAL WITH ANYTHING**!

Part 2: Crafting Your Unshakeable Foundation

Chapter 3: Goal Setting is Worse Than a Waste of Time

"If you have built castles in the air, your work need not be lost; that is where they should be. Now put the foundations under them." — Henry David Thoreau

If you've gotten this far in this book, by now you know, in fall of 2016 I left out the biggest dream of my life by riding a bicycle solo across the USA. Now, let *me* let *you* in on my dirty little secret: I'm not actually capable of riding a bicycle 3,000 miles to get across the country. Hell, up to that point, I'm not sure that I'd ever ridden that many miles in any single year!

The trouble with goals is people who set them focus on them.

Who am I to Take on a Guru Like Zig Ziglar

I'm going to bring up that story about Zig Ziglar from the preface of this book again. Back in 1992, I was brand new to sales and a coworker told me about Zig Ziglar and his unmatched motivational powers. I'd never even heard of this sales guru with the funny name before. But I was intrigued enough to buy a set of his cassette tapes. He turned out to be the most incredible motivator I'd ever heard. Right off the bat, he began preaching about the almost magical power of setting goals. I can still hear his thick, disarming Yazoo City, Mississippi accent as he said, "Ya got ta have them GOOOAAAALLLLLSSSS!" He went on to explain in those tapes, "When you set goals, something inside you starts saying, 'Let's go, let's go, let's go,' and ceilings start moving up."

If 'ole Zig was as completely right about goals as he was charming and disarming, every salesperson who ever bought his books or tapes would be rich, none would be fat, and there wouldn't be much of a need for books on resilience.

I know... I know... who the eff am I to take on one of the greatest selling and motivational legends the world has ever known? And, to be fair, Ziglar did talk about the importance of short-term goals too (which I think still falls short, just a little less short). But, in the words of Dan Kennedy, the world-renowned "No BS" marketing expert and legend in his own right, "If Zig Ziglar and I agreed on everything, the world wouldn't need both of us."

If you think I'm wrong when I say that "goal setting is worse than a waste of time," I invite you to visit any fitness center you choose in early January. You can hardly get in the door because it's so damn crowded. But by the 15th, it starts to thin out a little. By February 1st, the place is practically empty again. That's what New Year's resolutions (a.k.a. goal setting) gets you. When's the last time you or anyone you know actually achieved a New Year's resolution of any real significance?

It's not that Zig and goal setting are wrong—it's just that, much like the BE-DO-HAVE model, goal setting is incomplete. In fact, it's incomplete to the point of being worse than a waste of time if all you do is simply set goals. Even S.M.A.R.T. goal setting falls short... or way short, depending on how far you take it. The farthest I've seen a S.M.A.R.T. goal-setting session go is to break big goals down into smaller goals, which, admittedly, is a step in the right direction.

But the real solution can be summed up in one quote by James Clear, author of *Atomic Habits* (one of the most life-changing books I've ever read): "Goals are good for setting direction, but systems are best for making progress."

And to make it even clearer, he goes on to say, "You do not *rise* to the level of your goals. You *fall* to the level of your systems."

Even breaking down all goals into very bite-sized, short-term chunks typically overlooks one of the most insidious, psychologically poisonous qualities of goal setting: the reward is entirely tied to achieving the goal. This is where nearly everyone I've ever seen who coaches or facilitates goal-setting sessions starts to back-fill with concepts like accountability and motivation. Now, don't get me wrong, I'm 1,000% all for accountability. And good luck even getting out of bed each morning without some form of motivation. Both are critical ingredients in life, and both absolutely have their place. But in the context of goal setting, neither holds a ton of weight or value because it's rare that either is sustainable or focused for long.

Here's the thing: when you've done the work of creating processes that lead to the accomplishment of your goals, if done correctly, you naturally stay motivated. Why? Because the simple act of completing a step in the process becomes psychologically rewarding, knowing it's leading you to the ultimate goal. For example, I don't even think about my fitness goals anymore. I absolutely have them, but I enjoy and have so much confidence in the processes that get me there that I don't even need to think about the goal. I certainly don't need motivation or accountability to reach it.

Set Goals, Just Don't Start or Stop There

Short of putting this book down and picking up *Atomic Habits* instead of this chapter (which, by the way, I highly recommend you do—just don't forget to come back and finish *this* book!), let's break it down:

First and foremost, before you even set a goal, have an honest and unfiltered discussion with yourself. Ask, *Do I truly want to achieve this goal?* Then, and this part is critical, dig deep and ask yourself the most important question of all: *Why?*

Simon Sinek, celebrated for his book "Start With Why", often shares a story that illustrates the profound impact of beginning with purpose when setting goals. One of his most memorable examples involves the Wright brothers—Orville and Wilbur—and their pursuit of powered flight.

In the early 1900s, the Wright brothers faced stiff competition from Samuel Langley, a well-funded and highly respected inventor. Langley had significant financial backing from the U.S. government and access to the best minds and resources of the time. By contrast, the Wright brothers had no formal funding, working out of a modest bicycle shop in Dayton, Ohio, with a small and dedicated team.

So why did the Wright brothers succeed when Langley failed? According to Sinek, the difference lay in their "why." Langley was primarily motivated by fame and fortune. He sought recognition and prestige for being the first to achieve powered flight. The Wright brothers, on the other hand, were driven by a deep passion and a sense of purpose—they wanted to change the world by making flight accessible to everyone. Their *why* inspired relentless effort, innovation, and teamwork despite their limited means.

When Langley learned the Wright brothers had successfully flown, he abandoned his work altogether. His motivation vanished because his "why" was rooted in personal gain, not purpose.

Sinek uses this story to emphasize that when we start with "why," our goals become more meaningful and enduring. A clear "why" fuels persistence, inspires others to support our vision, and keeps us grounded during challenges. For anyone setting goals, the lesson is this: always connect your objectives to your deeper purpose. When the "why" is strong enough, the "how" and "what" will naturally follow

Once you've decided that the "juice is worth the squeeze," take your list of S.M.A.R.T. goals or BHAGs (Big Hairy Audacious Goals) and start reverse-engineering them. Assume from the start that unexpected obstacles and setbacks will arise—because they absolutely will, 100% of the time. Break the big goal into smaller sub-goals or KPIs (Key Performance Indicators—a fancy way of saying "the smaller milestones that move you closer to the bigger goal"). Keep breaking it down until you've identified at least one DMO (Daily Method of Operation—a similarly fancy term for the simple, repeatable daily processes that build toward achieving something significant) for each goal you set.

At this point, it's important to emphasize that everything in your DMO should be entirely within your control. If it's not (and here's a hint: outcomes are almost never fully within your control), it belongs either as a KPI or as something you shouldn't bother paying attention to at all.

At least at the beginning, your DMOs should be broken down to the most granular level possible—powder-fine, even. For example, let's go back to my fitness process (fitness being something that's extremely important to me). I'm a morning person—so much so that one friend once told me, "You don't get up in the morning. You get up in the middle of the night."

The first item on my weekday DMO is simple: my feet hit the floor at 4:50 a.m. That's it. And while it's straightforward, it can still be tough sometimes, even for a morning person like me. But here's the key—it's something I'm 100% in control of. Whether or not I get out of bed at 4:50 a.m. is entirely up to me.

Once I've accomplished that first step, I'm on autopilot. I don't have to overthink what comes next because the process is already set in motion. Over the years, I've learned that if I just get out of bed at 4:50 a.m. consistently, my fitness takes care of itself. In fact, I'll let you in on a little secret: I don't even have "fitness goals" anymore. I have fitness processes.

Here's an example that might resonate with salespeople: to hit your overall sales target, you probably know your monthly, weekly, and even daily sales goals. But instead of fixating on those numbers, shift your focus to the actions that drive those results—like the number of sales calls you need to make in a given timeframe.

Now, it does depend on how you define "sales call," because you're not in control of whether someone answers the phone, opens your email, or agrees to an appointment. Be mindful of this when deciding where to direct your mental and emotional energy. What *is* within your control? The number of times you dial the phone and the number of emails you actually send in a given time. Are both in your control. Also, the number of presentations you give is not in your direct control. But the quality of those presentations is in your control, so that should be a major focus.

From there, develop a metric or method—separate from closed sales—to evaluate the quality of those presentations. This is where I need to give a shout-out to my friend and mentor, Angel Salinas, a master sales professional and trainer with Sandler Sales in San Antonio, Texas. Angel teaches that every single aspect of your sales process must be systemized.

By focusing on the system and not just the outcome, you not only gain clarity but also maintain control over the variables that truly matter. That's where sustainable success lies.

Once you've done all of this, keep your overall goals in mind—but otherwise, forget about them. Focus entirely on your system, your process. Adopt the mindset that a day spent working within your system, achieving your DMOs, is a "W," no matter the results. Conversely, a day outside your system, failing to achieve your DMOs, is an "L," regardless of any short-term success.

I know what you're thinking: "All this DMO, KPI, BHAG, and SMART soup really complicates the hell out of everything." But here's the counterintuitive truth: this systematic way of managing your life actually simplifies the hell out of it.

Take my bike ride across the USA as an example. Let me remind you: I'm not actually capable of riding a bike 3,000 miles across the country. But here's the thing—I didn't have to be. What I *was* capable of was following a process.

The absolute first thing I did—four years before I even started the journey—was decide if this was something I really wanted to do. I got crystal clear on my *why*. Once I knew the juice was worth the squeeze, I created a plan. I made a list of everything that could go wrong on a trip like this—mechanical issues, injuries, bad weather, you name it—and figured out what I'd do if those things happened.

Then, when the journey began, my process was simple:

- Wake up around 6:30 AM and have breakfast.
- While eating, figure out where I'd stop for lunch and ride there.
- At lunch, decide where I'd sleep that night and ride to that spot.
- Aim to reach my dinner/sleep destination by 3:00 PM to leave plenty of wiggle room for unexpected problems (like breakdowns, weather, detours, or plain old fatigue).

- Before bed, sketch out a rough plan for the next day.

That's it. I repeated that process 60 times in a row. And just like that, I "magically" made it from San Diego, CA, across 8 states, 4 time zones, 2 deserts, and more mountain ranges than I can count, all the way to St. Augustine, FL.

Sure, my goal was to ride across the country—a textbook S.M.A.R.T. goal: Specific, Measurable, Attainable, Relevant, and Time-Bound. But here's the catch: had I focused solely on the *goal* itself, I'm 100% certain I would've quit within the first week.

What got me through wasn't the goal. It was the *system*. Because I was prepared on every level, 100% immersed in my process, and powered by an indelibly clear *why*, rolling with the punches felt easy.

Whether you're working to build resilience, improve your cardio, grow your bottom line, pedal a bike across the country, or beat a life-threatening illness, here's the deal: you need a process. Create a journey you can stick to—one you can tolerate at the very least, but ideally one you'll fall in love with. When you do that, you become unstoppable because you know, deep down, that **YOU CAN DEAL WITH ANYTHING***!*

Chapter 4: Alchemy of Action
"I must lose myself in action, lest I wither in despair" – Alfred Lord Tennyson

Around 1991, I stumbled across a cassette tape featuring Tony Robbins, who I think was still a relatively new phenomenon at the time. On that tape, Robbins interviewed a man named Paul Zane Pilzer. Pilzer, among his many accomplishments, had an impressive academic résumé, and the interview ended up being, to this day, one of the most fascinating I've ever heard.

There were several reasons it left such a lasting impression on me. One of the most striking was that, in this pre-Internet interview, Pilzer predicted the e-commerce world we now live in with an almost eerie level of accuracy. As he described the seismic opportunities that this "Internet thingy" was about to unleash, he framed it as the biggest revolution in goods and services distribution since the industrial revolution itself. And here's the kicker: in this same discussion, Pilzer essentially described Amazon—nearly to a "T"—even though Amazon wouldn't be founded for another three years!

Looking back, it's astonishing how spot-on his predictions were. Pilzer didn't just glimpse the future; he articulated it in a way that now feels like prophecy.

The heart of the interview was Pilzer's groundbreaking theory of "Economic Alchemy." (He had written a book in 1990 titled *Unlimited Wealth: The Theory and Practice of Economic Alchemy*. Pilzer challenged one of the most fundamental assumptions of economics: the idea that "the study of economics is the study of society's allocation of scarce resources." Pilzer argued that resources are not, in fact, scarce. Instead, he asserted that everything we consider a "resource" is a creation of the human mind—and since human imagination is unlimited, so too are our resources. Talk about an abundance mentality!

To illustrate his point, Pilzer shared a story about what we now regard as one of our most fundamental resources: land. In the era of hunter-gatherers, land wasn't considered a resource at all. In fact, when Europeans first arrived in the New World and introduced the concept of land ownership to Native Americans, the idea was laughable to them. Pilzer explained that Native Americans would humor the Europeans by saying something like, "Sure! We'll sell you our land, but we already killed all the buffalo on it and ate all the fruit off the trees." To them, it was like selling the wrapper of a candy bar they had already eaten.

It wasn't until human minds figured out how to farm the land and domesticate animals that it became a resource in the first place. Pilzer's point was clear: resources are born of human innovation, and the only real limit is our imagination.

Fail Forward. And Do So FAST!

To set the stage for explaining his theory in greater detail, Pilzer delved into the history of several key figures and concepts, including Aristotle, Galileo, and the history of alchemy. He explained the role of ancient alchemists and why they did what they did. The alchemists' primary goal was to find a way to produce more gold for the king by experimenting with common metals like lead, attempting to transform them into the far more valuable gold. Of course, their efforts to turn lead into gold were a complete failure. However, in their unsuccessful quest to convert base metals into precious ones, their work inadvertently laid the groundwork for the study of chemistry—and what would eventually become modern medicine.

Their failures, it turns out, were not in vain. In fact, had the alchemists been successful, their work would have likely just caused gold to lose its value. So it's highly arguable that their "failed" work to turn lead into gold ended up far more successful than it would have been had they succeeded!

I bring up Pilzer, his theory of economic alchemy, and even the ancient practice of actual alchemy because, over the years, I've realized that the overarching concept of alchemy has a profound impact on how we navigate everyday life—especially when it comes to dealing with failure.

That said, this chapter isn't specifically about failure, per se.

This chapter is about embracing the value of taking action, even when you don't have it all figured out. It's about recognizing that action—and its inevitable companion, failure—are not only the most efficient paths to success, but that they often unlock unexpected opportunities, even when the action ends in complete disaster.

One of my many toxic traits has always been a deep-seated fear of failure. The truth, though? Failure can be—and usually is—my best ally. I know I'm not alone in this. Like so many people, I have an ingrained tendency to want everything perfectly planned and polished before I make a move. But here's the kicker: that's not just flawed thinking—it's entirely backward.

For those in the small business or sales world, the value of failure is practically gospel. They know you've got to endure a lot of "no's" and rejection to eventually land a "yes." But when you really stop to think about it, failure goes far deeper than just being part of the sales process. It's not just a stepping stone to success—it's the bridge that gets you there.

In 2001, two years into my second attempt at carving out success in the financial services industry, I noticed a growing trend: large numbers of CPAs were beginning to add financial planning, investments, and insurance to their suite of services. This movement immediately caught my attention because, having been raised by a CPA, I understood three things with absolute certainty:

1. CPAs, for good reason, are often seen as their clients' most trusted advisors—the steady, reliable cornerstone in their network of professionals.
2. While many CPAs recognized the opportunity in expanding into financial planning, investments, and insurance, most would need to hire new staff and train them in areas where they themselves had little to no experience.
3. CPAs simply *think* differently. They have a unique approach to problem-solving and decision-making, and as a result, they also *speak* differently. For instance, you never say the word "commission" in the presence of a CPA—it's "revenue generated" or some equally measured term. Having grown up immersed in this world, I knew exactly how to communicate with CPAs and speak their language.

This understanding presented me with a rare opportunity I couldn't ignore.

I also discovered that the company I worked for was launching a corporate-level initiative to market to and recruit CPAs who were interested in adding financial planning services to their practices. Recognizing a massive opportunity, I began reaching out to CPAs to help them get into the game. The arrangement was straightforward: they would refer their clients to me, and after obtaining the necessary licensing, they could participate in the revenue generated. I would handle all the actual financial planning work in exchange for a share of that revenue.

To my excitement, the idea gained substantial interest among the CPAs I spoke with. I thought, *"If I can recruit just one CPA, it could be a career-defining moment!"* After a few dozen meetings with CPAs in my area, one particular meeting stood out. This guy and I clicked immediately. We were close in age, and there was a strong sense of "business chemistry" between us. Before long, he was ready to move forward, and I felt like everything was finally falling into place.

But then I discovered that the corporate-level initiative to recruit CPAs was not being warmly embraced in my local office. To say I was puzzled by my managers' resistance would be an understatement. While top management and I both saw this as a golden opportunity, my local leadership seemed to view it as nothing but a source of problems and complications. They didn't outright stop me from pursuing this path, but they sure didn't encourage it—or support me in any meaningful way.

As part of my efforts to recruit and vet the CPA I mentioned earlier, I arranged for him to come into the office to meet my managers and discuss the potential business relationship. Unfortunately, the meeting went about as poorly as I'd feared. It wasn't a total disaster, but my managers were lukewarm at best. It was painfully clear that they had no understanding of the CPA's world, nor any interest in trying to bridge that gap. Their lack of enthusiasm was impossible to ignore. Predictably, this caused my CPA prospect to start losing interest in working with me.

I was frustrated and disappointed, but I still saw enormous potential in this opportunity. Determined not to let it slip away, I decided to try an "end-around." After giving it considerable thought and doing some research, I arranged another meeting with the CPA. During our conversation, I asked him if my switching firms—or even going independent—might rekindle his interest in working together.

To my relief, he responded positively. He told me he had become comfortable with the idea of partnering with me and, from what little he knew about the financial services industry, he understood that the firm I worked for was largely an "interchangeable part." With that in mind, he agreed to keep the possibility open while I explored firms that might be more receptive to the approach we were trying to take.

It took over a year, but I eventually found a local outfit that specialized in serving as a "back-office support arm" for independent financial advisors and insurance agents. They not only fully understood the business arrangement we wanted to create but also enthusiastically embraced it. Their platform and suite of products and services were far larger and more robust than what my previous firm offered.

Because this new outfit was a support arm for independent advisors—not a "career shop"—their payout and commission percentages were significantly higher than those at my old firm. This was a game-changer. It meant the CPA and I would have access to a much broader range of products and services to offer his clients, enabling us to serve a wider variety of needs, especially those of clients with more sophisticated requirements. On top of that, we'd be splitting a substantially larger revenue pie in the process!

It's worth pointing out that, had I done my homework before taking action—specifically, discussing with local management my desire to forge alliances with CPAs—I would never have pursued the opportunity. The obstacles and lack of support from my office would have been enough to discourage me from even trying. But because I took the "ready, fire, aim" approach, my career reached a new level. Ironically, my initial effort was a complete failure, but that very failure paved the way for significant improvements in my overall situation on multiple fronts.

The intuitive approach in life is to figure everything out first and then take action. And sometimes, that's absolutely the right move! You don't climb into the cockpit of an airplane, take off, and *then* decide it's time to learn how to fly. Similarly, many of life's problems could be avoided if we just paused to think *before* opening our mouths. But too often—and I'm speaking from experience here—"thinking it through" becomes code for, *"I'm too scared to act."*

An Ounce of Action is Worth 10 Pounds of Brilliance

To truly put this concept into practice, you must translate your intentions into actual, tangible output. Without this step, your brain has a sneaky way of convincing you that you're taking massive action—even when, in reality, all you're doing is *thinking* about it.

I'll use the process of writing this very book and building the similarly themed speaking career and business I'm working on as an example. For years, I dreamed of becoming a speaker and author (remember that lowercase "do" we discussed back in Chapter 2?). I spent countless hours thinking about it, researching online, and reflecting on what I believed to be a shit-ton of great experiences and stories worth sharing. But I also knew a hard truth: besides me and a few close friends and family, nobody was going to care about stories that were all about *me*.

For a long time, I tricked myself into believing I was making progress just by *thinking* about my perfect message. But in reality, nothing started to take shape until I began getting in front of small audiences and actually *speaking*. That's when things started to click—and let me tell you, some of those early talks were absolute disasters.

What saved me was the clarity that only action brings. Watching what resonated (and what flopped) with those early audiences gave me insight into what my message needed to be and who would benefit most from it. Through trial and error, I realized my core themes needed to center around resilience and mindset. Market research backed this up, suggesting that these topics are "evergreen," meaning there's a consistent demand for them.

With that clarity, I could finally sit down and brainstorm what this book should look like. And almost like magic, the act of actually typing out content—just as I had been doing in those talks—opened a floodgate in my mind. Ideas that had been floating around for years suddenly aligned, and new ones emerged. These ideas weren't just about my experiences but how I could use them to genuinely help others—and, hopefully, build a business that not only supports me financially but also makes an impact on others' lives.

In the end, it wasn't all the thinking or planning that moved the needle—it was taking action, however imperfect, that brought it all together.

I find that the more I speak and the more I write, the better it all becomes—everything, including my strategies for how to use it all. But here's the truth: if I had just continued to think and research about the perfect speech and the perfect book, without actually putting my thoughts and ideas out into the world and on paper, I'd be completely stuck. And I'd know far less than I do now about the business of speaking and book publishing.

To be frank, as I'm typing this, I'm realizing that everything I'm working on is, at its core, just that: a work in progress. There's no guarantee it will help a single person or achieve the success I originally envisioned. But here's what I do know for sure: taking action, even imperfect action, will absolutely bring rewards—even if those rewards aren't what I initially expected. And there's a very good chance that my action will lead me to something even better than I originally anticipated!

I'm reminded of a story I read in the late 1980s in the *Indianapolis Star* about a guy named Mark Messner, an All-American defensive lineman from the University of Michigan. He was undersized, not particularly strong, and a little slow on his feet—by Big Ten football standards, at least. Yet, despite these physical shortcomings, he earned a starting spot as a freshman and went on to become the first player in Michigan's history to be named first-team All-Big Ten four years in a row, in addition to earning All-American honors. Even after 40 years, he still holds Michigan's career records for quarterback sacks and tackles for loss. In the article, he was asked how he managed such success when, by all normal standards, he didn't seem to have the physical gifts necessary. His reply has always stayed with me, and it's the reason I recall the article and the player in the first place: "I learned in my very first practice at Michigan that if I just kept my feet moving, good things just seemed to come my way." **READ THAT QUOTE AGAIN!!**

While "thinking before acting" definitely has its place and is the smartest approach in many contexts—if not most—having the courage to move forward before you have it all figured out often leads you to different destinations than you originally intended. And more often than not, those destinations turn out to be even better than what you had originally planned! This is one of the collateral benefits of placing the lowercase "do" in front of the "Be-Do-Have" model as discussed in Chapter 2.

As one of my mentors, Tim David, likes to say, "It's not 'clarity THEN action'. It's 'clarity VIA action'." Life rewards action, not intelligence or perfection. It's action!

If we can learn to take action, even in the face of great doubt and uncertainty, we will know that **WE CAN DEAL WITH ANYTHING**!

Chapter 5: Find/Discover/Know Your Purpose

"Efforts and courage are not enough without purpose and direction" -John F. Kennedy

The purpose of my life can be summed up in a three-word mantra: Adventure. Support. Inspire. I've embraced this mantra with clear intention for the past 12 years, and I believe anyone who knows me, even just a little, would understand it when they hear me describe my purpose in those three words. Yet, for the first 40 or so years of my life, the only purpose I had was immediate gratification. I wonder why I struggled so much?

Angel Salinas is a teacher at Hart, but his path took an unexpected turn into a sales career. Eventually, he found his true passion and calling—his purpose—by creating a sales training business in San Antonio, Texas. Originally from Monterrey, Mexico, Angel faced immense challenges in the early years of building his business, which he considers his baby.

"Thinking about resilience has always helped me understand that the only way you can embrace adversity is by finding meaning or purpose in doing what you have to do. That's what helped me through this journey—moving to this country from Mexico, not knowing anyone, starting a business from scratch, being exposed to a different culture, a different language... all that head trash. 'Why would anyone want to buy from me?' When I think about all the obstacles I faced and what I had to do to push through them, it was finding meaning and purpose that gave me that will." – Angel Salinas

Because Angel had a clear and deeply rooted sense of purpose, and because his work was ultimately aligned with that purpose—or at least he was able to tie his work to the bigger picture of what he truly cared about—he was able to maintain resilience in the face of extremely challenging circumstances.

For me, the creation of the Pancreatitis Foundation (which I co-founded alongside one of the doctors who treated me during a particularly difficult and life-threatening period with that disease) marked the very beginning of my journey toward discovering my own purpose. Then, my cross-country journey solidified it, giving me even more clarity on what I was truly meant to do.

But in between those moments, I would often forget about my purpose and slip back into the routine of simply trying to get through the day, the week, or the month—doing whatever provided me with the most immediate reward. This was when depression and anxiety would settle in.

I had an epiphany toward the end of my cross-country journey. I realized that I had found a way to take the painful, difficult experience of battling pancreatitis and use it to help someone else facing a similar struggle—turning my hardship into a blessing. So, when I was diagnosed with cancer, it didn't hit me with the devastation I might have expected. Instead, I saw it almost immediately as an opportunity to live out and fulfill my purpose. I just needed to survive long enough to make that happen. And my oncology team believes—just as I do—that tying my cancer diagnosis to my purpose has played an enormous role in helping me weather this storm as well as I have.

Ok, But How?

Discovering and creating your purpose is deeply personal. Angel and I have shared just a couple of examples to illustrate what that journey can look like. In my (admittedly biased) opinion, the best source material for uncovering your purpose lies within your own life—specifically, in the biggest challenges you've faced. There's absolutely no way you're the only one dealing with that problem. Find a way to help others who are navigating the same struggle, and you may just stumble upon your purpose in the process.

Here's a list of things you can think about which can act as exercises to help you with this extremely important task:

- Get the focus off what **you'll** get out of this!
- What are you most passionate about?
- Actually, forget your passion. What *burdens* you?
- What are your core values?
    - What B.S. do you have (belief systems)
        - Just be sure to identify and eliminate your **limiting B.S.**
- What unique or rare experiences have you had?
- Take inventory of your childhood influences and experiences.
- Think about your unique and skills.
- Explore your natural inclinations, and preferences.
- Talk with family and friends.
- What do people randomly approach you and ask you for advice about?
- Think about life, changing experiences and coincidences.
- Think like a leader (even if you're not)-a **servant** leader.
- Volunteer.

- Take a personality assessment.
- Ask yourself 3 questions:
    - What does it seem? I was born to do?
    - What does it seem my life has been leading up to?
    - What does it seem? I'm in the business of doing?
- Write your own epitaph
    - Then live up to it every day.
- Explore the intersection of what you love, what you're good at, what the world needs (**IKIGAI**), and what you can be paid for.

And the list goes on and on.

These days, if I can't tie what I'm doing back to my purpose—whether it's using my own pain as a way to help others with theirs or living out my *Adventure. Support. Inspire.* mantra—I make a conscious effort not to do it.

Research has consistently shown that having a clear sense of purpose can greatly enhance a person's ability to navigate and overcome adversity. Here are three notable studies that illustrate this powerful connection:

1. **Purpose in Life and Resilience Among College Students During COVID-19**: A study published in *Frontiers in Psychology* examined how life purpose influenced resilience and persistence in college students amid the challenges of the COVID-19 pandemic. The findings indicated that students with a well-defined sense of purpose exhibited higher levels of resilience and were more persistent in their academic

endeavors, suggesting that a clear purpose can buffer against the adverse effects of unprecedented challenges. (https://pmc.ncbi.nlm.nih.gov/articles/PMC8883129/?utm_source=chatgpt.com)

2. **Purpose in Life and Stress Reduction**: A meta-analysis discussed by the American Psychiatric Association found that individuals with a greater sense of purpose experienced lower levels of stress. This association was consistent across various demographics, including age, sex, race, ethnicity, and education levels (so don't think having a clear purpose won't help **you**), underscoring the universal benefit of having a clear purpose in mitigating stress responses. (https://www.psychiatry.org/news-room/apa-blogs/purpose-in-life-less-stress-better-mental-health?)

3. **Purpose in Life and Physical Health Outcomes**: Research highlighted by the University of Michigan's School of Public Health revealed that individuals with a strong sense of purpose not only tend to live longer but also approach life's challenges with healthier attitudes and behaviors. This suggests that a clear purpose contributes to better physical health and equips individuals to handle adversity more effectively. (https://sph.umich.edu/pursuit/2024posts/the-power-of-purpose-how-our-deepest-intentions-shape-our-health.html?)

These studies collectively highlight that having a well-defined life purpose acts as a powerful resource, boosting resilience, lowering stress, and encouraging healthier behaviors—all of which are essential for overcoming significant challenges and navigating adversity.

What a Hiker and Prisoner Can Teach Us about Purpose and Survival

One of the most extreme and compelling stories I've heard of **survival** fueled by purpose is that of Aron Ralston, whose harrowing ordeal became widely known through his autobiography *Between a Rock and a Hard Place* and the subsequent film *127 Hours*. His story is a powerful example of how having a clear purpose can help someone overcome life-threatening adversity.

In 2003, Aron, an experienced mountaineer, went hiking alone in the remote canyons of Utah. While descending into a narrow canyon, a boulder dislodged and trapped his right arm against the canyon wall. He was completely alone, with no way to signal for help and limited food and water. For five days, Aron struggled to free himself, but his efforts were futile.

As dehydration and despair set in, Aron reflected on his life. In that moment, his purpose crystallized: he wanted to survive so he could return to his family, contribute to the world, and tell his story to inspire others. This deep sense of purpose gave him the courage to do the unthinkable.

On the sixth day, Aron made the life-saving decision to amputate his own arm using a small, dull multi-tool. The process was excruciating, but his will to live—to fulfill his purpose—was stronger than the pain. After freeing himself, he trekked miles through the canyon, bleeding and exhausted, until he was found by rescuers.

Aron's survival was not just a testament to physical endurance but to the power of purpose. His unwavering vision of reuniting with his loved ones and living a meaningful life enabled him to overcome unimaginable pain and adversity.

Today, Aron shares his story as a motivational speaker, emphasizing the importance of purpose in overcoming life's challenges. His experience is a profound reminder that when we have a clear "why," we can endure almost any "how." This story could serve as a powerful narrative in your chapter, illustrating the life-saving impact of having a defined purpose.

Then there's Viktor Frankl, with whom I've dared to slightly disagree on his assertion that one can simply choose his mindset (please don't beat me up or sue me for this!)

The renowned psychiatrist and Holocaust survivor's story is perhaps the most legendary in history on this topic. His experience during World War II, as detailed in his influential book *Man's Search for Meaning*, is a powerful testament to the transformative power of having a clear purpose.

Frankl was imprisoned in several Nazi concentration camps, including Auschwitz, where he endured unimaginable suffering, including the loss of his entire family. Stripped of everything—his freedom, possessions, and even his dignity—Frankl observed that those who survived were not always the physically strongest but often those who had a clear sense of purpose.

For Frankl, his purpose became twofold: to survive so he could share his psychological insights with the world and to finish the manuscript he had been working on before his imprisonment. This deep sense of "why" gave him the mental resilience to endure starvation, extreme cold, and relentless labor. When others around him gave up hope, Frankl's purpose became his anchor, enabling him to find meaning even in the midst of suffering.

One pivotal moment came when Frankl was assigned to dig trenches in freezing conditions. As despair threatened to consume him, he imagined himself lecturing to future audiences about the psychological lessons he had learned in the camps. This vision reignited his determination and reminded him that his suffering was temporary, but his purpose was eternal.

After surviving the Holocaust, Frankl fulfilled his purpose by sharing his philosophy, which he called logotherapy. His message was simple yet profound: life's meaning is not something we discover passively but something we create by identifying our unique purpose and living in alignment with it.

Frankl's story demonstrates that even in the darkest circumstances, a clear life purpose can serve as a guiding light, providing strength, direction, and hope. Including this story in your chapter would inspire readers to reflect on their own purpose and understand its potential to help them overcome their greatest challenges.

A word of caution (and this is just my opinion): Your work and your family are typically not your purpose. I say this because both often feel like "default" answers, rooted in the idea of, "This is how I *should* answer the question, 'What is my purpose?'" However, if you feel differently on this point, I'd encourage you to run through at least some of the bullet points listed above to ensure your purpose truly resonates on a deeper level.

I'll leave you with one final thought on "purpose," and it's a sports analogy—or actually, two. In boxing, coaches teach fighters to punch through their opponents. Similarly, in football, defenders are instructed to tackle through their opponents. This technique adds power and precision, making their efforts far more effective.

I use these analogies because just a couple of weeks after my cancer diagnosis, I had lunch with two friends. During our conversation, I told them about my plans to speak, write a book, and help others once

I got through cancer. To be honest, I wasn't brimming with confidence that I'd survive long enough to make those dreams a reality. Still, both friends were surprised—almost shocked—by my post-illness plans. One of them remarked, "Wow, by making plans for life after cancer, you're taking the fight to the bully." (There's another analogy for you.)

It's this relentless focus—not on the problem itself, but on the purpose behind the problem—that instills in your mind the belief that **YOU CAN DEAL WITH ANYTHING**!

Part 3: ("T.R.A.S.H.") Your Daily Dose of Resilience

Tactical Vulnerability
Radical Responsibility
Attitude Aerobics
Supportive Village
Healing Humor

Chapter 6 My T.R.A.S.H.y Self-Discovery

"The desire for more positive experience is itself a negative experience. And, paradoxically, the acceptance of one's negative experience is itself a positive experience" - Mark Manson

Resilience, positive attitude, and mental toughness—three words and phrases I often use interchangeably—are not qualities we're simply born with. They must be acquired, earned through effort and experience. And this, I believe, is a good thing, supported by one expert's perspective.

Psychologist Carol Dweck's work on mindsets reveals that individuals who embrace a *growth mindset*—the belief that abilities and traits can be developed through effort—are more likely to face challenges head-on and persevere through setbacks. This perspective fosters resilience and a positive outlook, emphasizing that these traits can be nurtured rather than being fixed at birth (https://en.wikipedia.org/wiki/Carol_Dweck?).

To me, this distinction is critical. While some people may seem naturally gifted with these qualities, I think they're the exception, not the rule. Interestingly, Dweck points out that those with an innate tendency toward resilience or positivity might also lean toward a *fixed mindset*—believing that their abilities, intelligence, or talents are static traits they don't need to cultivate further. This raises an intriguing question: Could it actually be better in the long run to start life with a less-than-ideal mindset and develop these traits over time? Dweck's research suggests that might be the case.

I can personally attest to this. I sure as hell wasn't born with a good attitude. Growing up, I lacked mental toughness and resilience in every sense of the word. I had to learn and build those qualities brick by brick, through trial and error—and often through failure.

A great story which illustrates this point is Sara Blakely, the founder of Spanx. Sara started her career selling fax machines door-to-door. The job was grueling, filled with daily rejection, and Blakely often doubted herself. She struggled with a negative mindset, frequently thinking she wasn't smart enough or capable enough to achieve her dreams. These thoughts were reinforced by societal pressures and her own fears of failure.

One day, during a particularly difficult sales stretch, Blakely remembered advice from her father, who used to ask her and her brother at the dinner table: *"What did you fail at today?"* Her father reframed failure as a positive learning experience. This memory sparked a shift in her mindset. She realized her fear of failure was holding her back and that she needed to embrace failure as part of growth. Blakely began deliberately practicing positive self-talk and reframing challenges as opportunities. She used her door-to-door sales experience to build resilience and started focusing on what she *could* do rather than what she feared. This mental shift gave her the courage to pursue her idea for Spanx—a revolutionary undergarment product.

When she began pitching Spanx, she faced countless rejections. Manufacturers and investors dismissed her idea, claiming it was unworkable or niche. In the past, these rejections might have derailed her. Instead, Blakely leaned into her newfound positive mindset, viewing each "no" as one step closer to a "yes." She refused to let negativity define her journey and stayed laser-focused on her vision. Blakely's positive mindset not only helped her persevere but also enabled her to think creatively. For example, when she couldn't get a meeting with buyers, she found ways to connect directly with department stores, personally pitching her product and educating store associates to create demand. Her optimism and persistence paid off when Oprah Winfrey named Spanx one of her favorite products, propelling the brand into the spotlight.

Today, Sara Blakely is a billionaire and a self-made success story. She attributes much of her journey to the mental work she did to overcome negativity and embrace positivity. Blakely often speaks about the importance of mindset in business and life, saying, *"Failure is not the outcome—failure is not trying. Don't be afraid to fail.* Blakely's transformation shows that a negative mindset can be overcome with deliberate effort, self-awareness, and a focus on reframing challenges. Her story demonstrates how positivity doesn't just make obstacles bearable; it can turn them into opportunities for growth and success. I say it's also evidence that making a **transformation** such as the one Sara did actually gives one even more strength than they would have otherwise had. And this to cement the belief in one's mind that **THEY CAN DEAL WITH ANYTHING.**

The hard truth about resilience—like any worthwhile skill—is that it takes time and effort to develop. The good news? By intentionally adopting a daily, weekly, monthly, and even lifetime regimen based on the principles outlined in the upcoming chapters, you can build your "resilience muscle" no matter where you currently are in life. And, much like the roof of a house, the best time to strengthen it is before you desperately need it.

Now, even if you happen to be one of those "unlucky" souls who never faces significant adversity, let me assure you—applying these principles won't make your life worse. In fact, when I say "unlucky," I mean it sincerely. Facing and overcoming adversity is an essential part of the human experience. It's through navigating challenges that we grow, build character, and, perhaps most importantly, learn to truly appreciate the "good times." Even if there were no research to support this, I'd stand by the claim: the biggest challenges often create the most meaningful rewards.

The Single Biggest Turning Point of My Life

On August 11, 2022, I found myself lying in a bed in the ER at Northeast Baptist Hospital in San Antonio, TX. A doctor entered the room, introduced himself, and got straight to the point: "I can't give you an exact diagnosis because we haven't biopsied anything yet. But I've reviewed your CT scan, and I've been doing this a long time—I know what I'm looking at. You've got colon cancer. It's stage four. It's in your liver, too."

He proceeded to explain, from a high-level perspective, what treatment would likely involve and even offered a few words of encouragement. But then he dropped the hammer: "We'll deal with the cancer soon enough. The tumor in your colon has completely closed it off, so our first priority is to get you into surgery. If we don't, your colon will rupture, and you'll die."

His delivery was so direct, so devoid of sugarcoating, that it momentarily took me aback. But at the same time, I found myself strangely relieved. I appreciated the honesty, the clarity, and his no-nonsense approach. Over the years, I've heard countless stories from others who were given similar life-altering news—how it felt like the air was sucked from their lungs, how their world seemed to collapse in an instant. But I didn't feel any of that. Not even a little.

The reason for this lies in something we've already touched on—and will continue to discuss in this book—my *why*. That deep, driving purpose that keeps me grounded, no matter what. In that moment, as I absorbed the reality of my diagnosis, two things became crystal clear:

this cancer might very well kill me, but I wasn't afraid. I knew I could handle it. I knew, beyond a shadow of a doubt, that I COULD DEAL WITH ANYTHING!

My first real thought that morning was, How am I going to break this news to my mom and my two adult daughters? As soon as the doctor left the room, I called each of them one by one. I was pretty straightforward with them, but I also tried to downplay the situation a bit. I told them to be prepared for the worst, but I didn't want to overwhelm them. Each conversation ended with me asking them to keep the diagnosis quiet for the time being. I said, "This is my thing to deal with. We'll handle it as a family. But the last thing I want is for this shit to end up on Facebook."

About three days later, while I was still in the hospital, my mom called with a situation. My dad had passed away nine years earlier, and now she was getting remarried, with the wedding just a couple of weeks away. She said, "You're clearly not going to be here for my wedding, so if I'm supposed to keep your cancer diagnosis quiet, how do I explain your absence?" It was against my better judgment, but I ended up typing out a lengthy post detailing my situation and diagnosis. It was meant to be my one and only public comment, and I intended it to be shared only to ensure there would be no rumors circulating about my absence at my mom's wedding.

After typing everything out, I just didn't feel right about hitting "post." I stared at my phone for a couple of minutes, wrestling with myself, but eventually, I hit the button. Within maybe two minutes, my Facebook page and phone were flooded with an overwhelming outpouring of dozens—maybe even hundreds—of messages wishing me well and offering various forms of support. Many of these messages came from people I barely knew or hadn't spoken to in decades. I always thought I was someone who was good at making friends, yet I had lost touch with nearly all of them. But, as it turned out, even though I had just been thrust into the fight of my life, I discovered I had a much larger village behind me than I ever realized.

The encouragement and support I was receiving felt absolutely amazing. The outpouring from my village gave me the strength to resolve to fight this disease with everything I had—harder than I could have ever imagined. It made me want to set an example of how a person in my situation should handle such adversity, and it inspired me to live up to that example every single day—even when nobody else knew I was doing it.

As I navigated the early weeks of my diagnosis, I began reconnecting with so many friends and family. Nearly all of them commented on how, despite the diagnosis I had just received, my attitude seemed to be in the right place. With all of the kindness and encouragement I was receiving, how could I not have the perfect mindset? I genuinely had no fear whatsoever.

Don't get me wrong. I knew that my future was, at best, one big question mark, and I fully understood that whatever lay ahead would be difficult in ways I couldn't even fathom. But, despite that, I genuinely relished and looked forward to the challenge of it all.

Instead of asking, "Why me?", I was saying, "Thank God, me!"

I saw my cancer diagnosis as a challenge for which life had prepared me exceptionally well. I viewed the entire situation as an opportunity. The next two years would be nothing short of an absolute *motherfucker* at times, but they also turned into the best two years of my life.

I knew my mindset was in the right place for this fight, but I wasn't exactly sure how that happened, especially considering how poor my mindset used to be. I would often be derailed by even the smallest problems. So, I did a lot of self-reflection, asking myself when, where, why, and how my perspective had shifted. How had I evolved? How had I **TRANSFORMED**?

My family has always been amazing, but I came to a realization: without even realizing it, I had been building an incredible network of friends, starting all the way back to my teens and even earlier. My village had been in place all along!

But then, I started thinking and asking myself, "What have I been doing in the last few years that I wasn't doing earlier in my life? What have I been doing better?"

After much self-reflection, I realized there were five specific principles I had adopted and perfected over the years that helped me weather this and many other storms in my more recent years. These five principles—**T**actical Vulnerability, **R**adical Responsibility, **A**ttitude Aerobics, **S**upportive Village, and **H**ealing Humor (T.R.A.S.H.)—are fully teachable and learnable. Together, these five principles form what I now refer to as the "Resilience Regimen." Each one will be discussed in detail over the next five chapters.

None of us can predict the specific challenges or problems we'll face in life. But one thing is certain: major problems, pain, and adversity will inevitably come into our lives—and that's assuming they haven't already! What I do know for sure is that these five principles, when followed intentionally, can make you far more resilient and mentally tough than you ever imagined. I, myself, stumbled into the Resilience Regimen by accident over a long period of time.

However, by choosing to live these principles as an intentional lifestyle (and thereby shortening the timeline), you can completely transform your life. Doing so will help you cultivate an unshakeable mindset that tells you, without a doubt, **YOU CAN DEAL WITH ANYTHING**!

Chapter 7: Tactical Vulnerability

"Vulnerability is our most accurate measure of courage."
— Brené Brown

Vulnerability is a strength, not a weakness. It's also a skill that can be cultivated over time. What I call "Tactical Vulnerability" has two distinct sides to it—but let's not get ahead of ourselves just yet.

The best way to set the stage for this conversation—which is ultimately about courage, taking risks, and stepping out of your comfort zone—is to share the story of someone I believe is the true "Godmother" of empathy and vulnerability.

Brené Brown was a high-achieving academic who, like many of us, initially saw vulnerability as a weakness. As a social worker and researcher, she spent years studying how people experience connection, love, and belonging. Her work led to a startling realization: vulnerability—defined as uncertainty, risk, and emotional exposure—wasn't a weakness at all. In fact, it was the very foundation of courage, authenticity, and meaningful relationships.

This discovery sparked a personal reckoning for Brown. Despite her professional success, she struggled with perfectionism and a deep aversion to emotional exposure in her own life. She described this moment as a "breakdown," though she later reframed it as a "spiritual awakening." It was a turning point that forced her to confront the emotional armor she had spent years building to shield herself from vulnerability.

Brené Brown made the bold decision to embrace vulnerability by sharing her findings—and her own struggles—with the world. In her now-legendary TED Talk, *The Power of Vulnerability,* she spoke with raw honesty about her research and her personal journey to accept imperfection and lean into uncertainty. Her openness struck a powerful chord with millions, catapulting her talk to become one of the most viewed in TED history. The experience was transformative. By exposing her fears and flaws, Brown didn't just connect with her audience; she inspired them to redefine vulnerability as a source of strength.

Brown's message was simple yet profound: vulnerability isn't about weakness or oversharing—it's about showing up, being seen, and having the courage to risk failure, rejection, or criticism in the pursuit of something meaningful.

Her newfound vulnerability, however, came with its own challenges. After her TED Talk went viral, she faced waves of criticism and backlash, triggering old fears of judgment. But instead of retreating, she leaned deeper into her values of authenticity and resilience. She turned the criticism into fuel for growth, using it as an opportunity to connect even more deeply with her audience. Brown's response demonstrated her belief that resilience is built not by avoiding vulnerability, but by embracing it fully.

Today, Brené Brown is a leading voice in the fields of resilience, leadership, and emotional intelligence. Her bestselling books, including *Daring Greatly* and *Braving the Wilderness,* have inspired individuals and organizations to view vulnerability as the foundation for trust, innovation, and meaningful relationships. Her journey shows us that vulnerability isn't a liability—it's a superpower.

By embracing vulnerability, we can break down walls, build stronger connections, and develop the courage to tackle life's toughest challenges. Brown's story is a testament to the fact that resilience, a positive mindset, and mental toughness are not built by avoiding vulnerability but by stepping into it wholeheartedly—with an open heart and a willingness to grow.

Psychologists Agree With Brown

There's a mountain of scientific research out there proving that Brené Brown and I aren't just blowing anecdotal smoke. One notable study delves into the connection between vulnerability, character strengths, and psychological resilience, shedding light on just how essential these traits are for navigating life's challenges.

Research on vulnerability, character strengths, and psychological resilience explores how embracing one's vulnerabilities can lead to the development of character strengths, which in turn boost resilience and overall mental well-being. Character strengths, as defined by positive psychology, include traits like courage, perseverance, humility, gratitude, and self-regulation. The findings suggest that recognizing psychological vulnerabilities—such as fear, insecurity, or emotional exposure—creates a unique opportunity for growth.

(Quick sidebar: as I'll dive into later, intentionally creating situations that bring about these feelings, rather than just acknowledging them, can be an incredible way to harness their transformative power.)

This process requires self-awareness and authenticity, which are key to cultivating character strengths. For instance, someone who confronts their fear of failure may develop the courage to take calculated risks, ultimately fostering both confidence and resilience. The study highlights how embracing vulnerability isn't a weakness but a strategic step toward building a stronger, more adaptable mindset.

Character strengths serve as protective factors, shielding individuals from the damaging effects of stress and adversity. Embracing vulnerability often leads to reflective practices, such as seeking support or setting meaningful goals, which naturally cultivate strengths like perseverance and hope. For example, someone grappling with self-doubt might turn to gratitude practices, focusing on the support they've received from friends or mentors. This, in turn, deepens their sense of connection and bolsters their resilience.

(Quick note: we'll take a deep dive into this specific concept in Chapter 9, so stay tuned!)

Embracing vulnerability paves the way for greater authenticity, a quality deeply connected to the development of character strengths. Authenticity means aligning your actions with your core values and beliefs, even when it feels uncomfortable or risky. This alignment nurtures traits like integrity and humility—qualities essential for cultivating strong relationships and personal resilience.

Authentic vulnerability—whether it's admitting mistakes or reaching out for help—can also strengthen trust and empathy in relationships. This, in turn, fosters a supportive social network (more on this in Chapter 10) that becomes a critical pillar of resilience, helping you face life's challenges with greater confidence and strength.

A surprising finding from the research is that individuals who embrace vulnerability often exhibit greater optimism. By facing challenges head-on and acknowledging the potential for failure, they transition from a mindset of avoidance to one of possibility. This shift fuels strengths like hope and creativity, empowering them to navigate uncertainty with a proactive attitude.

Deliberately practicing vulnerability—such as admitting struggles or fears of judgment—fosters the development of strengths like courage and humility. These qualities, in turn, enhance an individual's capacity to manage future challenges more effectively. Leaders who embrace vulnerability can model transparency and authenticity, inspiring their teams to cultivate trust, resilience, and collaboration. In such environments, individuals feel empowered to bring their strengths to the table, driving collective growth and innovation.

This research underscores the transformative power of vulnerability in fostering character strengths. By embracing vulnerability, individuals open doors to greater authenticity, courage, and resilience, demonstrating that true strength often emerges from acknowledging and confronting our limitations. This approach not only accelerates personal development but also strengthens relationships and communities. It reveals vulnerability as a profound asset in enhancing both individual and collective well-being. (https://go.gale.com/ps/i.do?id=GALE|A682856345&issn=10461310&it=r&linkaccess=abs&p=HRCA&sid=googleScholar&sw=w&v=2.1&utm_source=chatgpt.com&userGroupName=anon~6e5a2e7d&aty=open-web-entry)

The Gift Which Made This So Real

For the practical purpose of this book—focused on resilience, positive mindset, and mental toughness—let's break down how vulnerability can be leveraged tactically to help you fully understand that **YOU CAN DEAL WITH ANYTHING**!

My 2016 cross-country bicycle ride (yes, I know, I keep bringing it up—but trust me, it's for good reason!) was the single greatest gift I've ever received. On the surface, it was the realization of the biggest dream I've ever dared to pursue. But it didn't stop there. This journey gave me so much: unforgettable memories, stories I'll carry forever, lifelong friendships, and a sense of accomplishment that's hard to put into words. Living out this adventure would have provided me with all of those things on its own.

But here's the thing: because I was fortunate enough to pursue this dream as a philanthropic mission, every single good thing about it was amplified tenfold. By tying my personal goal to something larger than myself, I unlocked a deeper level of meaning, connection, and fulfillment that I couldn't have imagined beforehand.

What truly made it the greatest gift I've ever received was the courage and vulnerability of the Theisen family from Noblesville, IN. They allowed their need for financial assistance to become a public story, openly sharing their struggles for the sake of their 3-year-old daughter, who was battling pancreatitis and in need of life-saving surgery. Their willingness to share their challenges gave my "magic carpet ride" of an adventure a deeper purpose, transforming it into something far more meaningful than I could have ever imagined.

By accepting help in such a brave and selfless way, they not only gave their daughter a fighting chance—they also gave me the single greatest opportunity and gift of my life. And make no mistake: it took a massive amount of courage for them to do this.

That journey was never about me. It was about that family—how they faced a heartbreaking situation with grace and turned it into a gift for so many others. It was about their bravery in asking for help the right way, showing that vulnerability, when coupled with strength and purpose, can create something truly extraordinary.

Like the earlier version of Brené Brown, our society has a deeply ingrained tendency to frown upon admitting we don't have our shit completely together—unless, of course, we can cloak it in a layer of victimhood (which I'll tackle head-on in the next chapter). Then, ironically, we seem all too eager to embrace it. We've trained ourselves to believe that complete self-sufficiency is the ultimate flex.

In sales and business especially, we go out of our way to project an image of being all-knowing, all-capable, perfectly polished, and practically bulletproof. But here's the thing: we'd be so much better off understanding that, as humans, we are hardwired to want to help others in need. By pretending we've got it all figured out, we deny ourselves the opportunity to connect with others in a genuine way—and we rob others of the chance to step up and show their care, strength, and support.

Don't believe me? Try this: on your next cold call, skip introducing yourself or your company right away. Instead, start with, *"I wonder if you can help me? I'm not sure I've called the right place. Can I take 30 seconds to explain the reason for my call, and then maybe you can point me in the right direction?"*

Even though the person answering the phone is likely paid and trained to sniff out and shut down salespeople, just see what happens when you approach them by asking for help first. You'll find that nearly 100% of the time, they'll be receptive, willing to listen, and eager to figure out how they can assist you.

Now, compare that to the typical sales approach: *"Hi, I'm the happiest person on earth, I'm completely awesome, and so is my company! Together, we can solve all your problems!"* This method—while intuitive for many salespeople—often leads to getting hung up on before they've even had a chance to explain why they called. Asking for help flips the script entirely, breaking through defenses and building connection right from the start.

I've learned that very few people truly connect with us when they perceive us as "awesome" (unless we've reached some kind of celebrity status—then all bets are off). In most cases, people are drawn to us and feel a genuine connection because, in our presence, *they* feel like *they're* awesome.

I call this "tactical" vulnerability for a reason. It's a deliberate reminder that vulnerability—like the other four pillars of the Resilience Regimen—should be used with intention. Vulnerability is a powerful and valuable tool in your resilience toolkit. But, just like any other tool, if it's used incorrectly, it won't just lose its effectiveness; it can also create bigger problems than it solves.

The Brené Brown story and the research study highlighted how vulnerability can be harnessed to strengthen your internal mindset and unlock its social power. Now, let's dive into the "how" of using vulnerability to seek help from others effectively.

One of my many toxic traits in life has been my reluctance to ask for help. It's been a struggle for me since childhood. I've either outright refused to seek help for fear of looking foolish or weak—an ironic mindset because *that* is the very definition of foolishness and weakness. Or, I've sought help from a place of victimhood.

Asking for help from a place of victimhood isn't true vulnerability. It's a form of manipulation—dumping your problems onto others or the world at large and expecting them to solve everything for you... or just plain whining. Let's be real: dumping and whining are rarely about genuinely solving a problem. They don't foster resilience, and they certainly don't tap into the power of vulnerability we've discussed so far.

Sure, playing the victim might earn you some short-term sympathy points from certain people. But in the long run, it leaves you stuck in the same mess—or worse. And here's the kicker: the people who *could* truly help you? They're usually the ones who will eventually distance themselves. Why? Because no one likes to feel like a dumping ground for someone else's unresolved issues.

The correct way to authentically use the power of vulnerability to seek help effectively boils down to three key principles. Think of it like your old boss's policy: "Don't come to me with a problem unless you also have a proposed solution." Of course, life is full of unique and nuanced situations, so think of this as a *framework*, not a rigid recipe.

1. **Be upfront, clear, and specific about what you need help with.** Never beat around the bush! If you're vague or hesitant, people may not even understand what you're asking for, let alone feel inspired to help.

2. **Communicate the effort you've already made or what you're bringing to the 'solution table.'** Share what you've done to address the issue or how you plan to contribute to the solution moving forward. This shows that you're not looking for a handout—you're seeking collaboration or support to get over a hurdle you're actively working to overcome.

3. **Be ready to compensate for the help you receive—when appropriate.** Compensation doesn't always mean money (though sometimes it does, and you need to be willing to pay for expertise). At the very least, always reciprocate value for value. This could mean offering help in return, sharing your gratitude in a meaningful way, or paying it forward to someone else. Whatever form it takes, gratitude must be expressed—100% of the time.

And remember, sometimes "paying it forward" is often even more powerful than "paying it back."

Don't say something like, *"I'm sad/upset/disappointed/frustrated because I have this big problem, and I just can't figure it out. I wish the big, mean world that's been taking advantage of me for so long would finally be nice and send a benevolent angel to magically fix everything for me at no cost, no effort, and no risk on my part."*

You may laugh, but let's be honest—you've seen people put this kind of stuff out there. Maybe it was during a conversation with family or friends, an email to a boss or coworker, or, most cringe-worthy of all, a social media post.

Instead, **do this**:

Say something like, *"I'm working my butt off to bring value to the world"* (assuming it's true, of course). *"Here's the specific value I'm bringing or striving to bring… Here's the work I've already put in so far…"* (Be clear and specific about your efforts and contributions to the solution.) *"Where I'm falling short is here… and the very specific help I need is this…"*

Take full responsibility for the problem, and when someone even *attempts* to help, express genuine gratitude or pay it forward. If the help you're receiving is from someone working within their professional expertise, **expect to pay them fully** for their services. NEVER ask for, expect, or even hint at wanting freebies or discounts in these situations.

As mentioned earlier, this is a nuanced conversation, and applying this side of Tactical Vulnerability will look different in every situation. However, the core elements—upfront clarity, specificity, communicating your ownership and responsibility, and offering compensation—should remain consistent across the board. Understand that, while people are generally drawn to help those who show vulnerability, they are often even more motivated to assist those who balance that vulnerability with a sense of strength and confidence.

This is exactly what the Theisen family did so beautifully. Their approach wasn't so much a direct request for help as it was an acceptance of it (keep in mind what I said about nuance). They made it clear to their village and to the world that they were facing financial challenges, but they did so in a way that perfectly aligned with the principles we're discussing here.

Comfort Zones Are Nice But Nothing Ever Grows There

As mentioned in the very first paragraph of this chapter, Tactical Vulnerability has two sides to it. Everything discussed so far covers the first side, but now let's explore the second side: placing yourself in situations that push you out of your comfort zone, and recognizing the growth opportunity presented when you find yourself in difficult circumstances that are beyond your control and were not of your choosing.

An extreme example for me is my battle with pancreatitis. As brutal and painful as that time in my life was, it prepared me incredibly well for when my cancer diagnosis came along. By then, I had no fear of death. I had become very comfortable with being uncomfortable, especially in the medical sense. Over time, I had built up a wealth of mental evidence that my body tends to respond positively to therapies and treatments. This single point became an enormous mental asset during that process, and it applies to everything in life.

Whether we're talking about a problem that's not of your making or an intentional effort toward growth, getting outside your comfort zone is one of the most beautiful, albeit often scary and awkward, places you can be! Angel Salinas (from Sandler Training in San Antonio) once said, with a laugh, "If someone says, 'I love adversity,' I would question whether they've really been in those types of situations." Now, I know Angel said that in a "tongue-in-cheek" way, and I completely understand what he really meant by it. But, I also need to take the rare opportunity to poke a little fun at him.

Adversity and stepping outside your comfort zone are usually not fun in the moment. Yet, once you've developed a truly resilient mindset, these situations should literally excite the holy crap out of you because you recognize the growth that's either happening or is about to happen.

In sales, having a really good mentor is, without question, one of the most valuable things in the world. When I was brand new to the financial services business, I was too young and too green at both business and life to be taken seriously by anyone. But I was fortunate enough to have a truly great mentor in a man named Rob Abernathy. He saw potential in me, took me under his wing, and joined me in all of my client meetings. He allowed me to literally screw everything up, only to swoop in and save me from my own mistakes. Then, he would debrief me after each meeting, pointing out everything I did right while also highlighting areas I needed to work on. He knew I'd screw up, and I knew I'd screw up. And that was the whole point!

I was scared shitless in most of those meetings. Not only was I a fumbling buffoon in front of prospective clients, but I was also that way in front of my new boss. I gained more skills, understanding of sales, and self-awareness—both of my strengths and weaknesses—during my first year with Rob than at any other time in my selling career.

Now, let's circle back one more time to my cross-country biking adventure to make this point: being loaded down like a Sherpa, riding at a snail's pace, and doing so in parts of the country I'd never been to before made me about as vulnerable as a person could be. I'd spent years getting myself ready for this moment, but still, riding away from the beach in San Diego, CA to start that journey, wondering what might happen to me out there, was among the scariest moments of my life. Yet, during that entire 3,000-mile trek, all I experienced were people going out of their way to perform acts of kindness for me and a 3-year-old little girl from Indiana, whom they'd likely never meet.

I remember thinking, just a couple of weeks into this adventure, while getting a little lost in Tucson, AZ, "It's crazy that this doesn't bother or scare me!" I could physically feel my comfort zone expanding!

I've reached a point where I can look anyone in the eye and say with confidence that my life has been anything but easy. But I can also say it's been nothing short of amazing. And I can't think of a single blessing in my life that can't be traced back to a difficulty I've faced or forced myself into at some point.

Vulnerability—true, authentic vulnerability—when handled the right way, draws people toward you in ways that having your shit completely together never will. And it also presents to you, usually in the simple form of life experience, the greatest teacher in the world.

We cyclists have a saying: "If the going seems easy, there's a good chance you're going downhill."

So don't just "embrace the suck," as the saying goes—use it! And when you do, you'll know, without a doubt, that **YOU CAN DEAL WITH ANYTHING!**

Chapter 8: Radical Responsibility

"Life is simple. Everything happens for you, not to you. Everything happens at exactly the right moment, neither too soon nor too late. You don't have to like it... it's just easier if you do." -Byron Katie

If this were the only chapter you read in this book, I would have made my greatest point.

Warning: I'm about to piss a lot of people off in this chapter, because I'm going to take away something they may or may not "love"—but something that certainly gives a lot of people a sense of comfort, and even power.

Keep reading.

In the spring of 2016, my life—which I had already made pretty challenging due to the choices I made in the first 50 years—began to fully unravel. Looking back, I realize I had unknowingly started making significant progress toward a better perspective, mental toughness, and resilience, but at the time, I wasn't being intentional about it. For me, many old "victimhood mentality" habits were still deeply rooted. A combination of health issues from pancreatitis, my failure to properly plan for such adversity, the 2008 economic crisis (which created a tough environment for everyone in the financial services industry), and regulatory challenges in my area of expertise, which shut down my most significant income stream, all created the perfect storm. This forced me to shut down my practice in 2010 and leave the industry completely the following year. And now, it was all coming to a head.

My pancreatitis was caused by a congenital defect in my biliary duct, making me highly prone to that awful disease. But I had also been self-medicating with alcohol for most of my life, and alcohol consumption is a known major risk factor for pancreatitis. The truth is, I was doing a lot of self-medicating, including with sugary foods. In 2012, I contracted bacterial meningitis. Once I had that under control, I found out that I was type II diabetic. I'm pretty certain that all of my health issues were largely fed—if not caused—by my habit of self-medicating with sugar and booze.

After shutting down my financial practice, I found myself bouncing from job to job, directionless and unsure of my purpose. If I had one, I sure as hell didn't know what it was. I was like a rudderless ship, drifting through life, and once again, I sank into a deep depression.

Then, more than two years after leaving the financial services industry, one of my clients named me in a lawsuit, accusing me and several others of fraud. There are plenty of negative words that could accurately describe me, but "fraud" or "fraudster" have never been among them. Hell, I'm the guy who was once mockingly referred to by one of my managers in the financial industry as "Honest Abe." But I sure as hell felt like a fraud when I was served those lawsuit papers! To this day, my stage-four cancer journey, with all its trials and hardships, feels like a walk in the park compared to the trauma of reading my name and what I was accused of in that lawsuit. The damn suit was thrown out of court nearly immediately, but the plaintiff refiled it, only for it to be tossed again. They didn't give up though— they refiled one more time and found a judge who agreed to let them move forward and, well, extort me... I mean, agreed that this frivolous lawsuit should be heard. So, for the next four years, I found myself consumed with it.

The one and only thing in my existence that I felt was on solid footing was my 27-year marriage. I thought my chances of being swept away by a tsunami in Central Indiana were greater than seeing my marriage crumble. But even that began to unravel in early 2016.

I felt angry. I felt bitter. I felt alone. I felt scared. I felt as though I was at rock bottom, a low place even for me!

Then, a massively important realization hit me.

I don't recall the exact date, but it was in the pre-dawn hours one morning in the first week of April 2016, just days after I learned that my marriage was coming to an end. I was driving through downtown Indianapolis when suddenly, a thought hit me like a stack of bricks. For the very first time in my life (at that point, 50 years of it), I knew that I completely owned myself! I was about to get a clean canvas! There was nobody on earth to whom I had to answer!

I've never been a "people pleaser," but so many of the significant choices I had made in my life—from going to college to the career path I chose, to where I lived, even the car I drove—had all been largely driven by what others in my life wanted for me, not what I wanted for myself. From this point forward, I would get to captain my own ship! I honestly felt like, **I CAN DEAL WITH ANYTHING**!

Freedom, Ownership & Empowerment's Inconvenient Fourth Partner

Freedom is an incredible thing. But it comes with a massive price: Responsibility. Not just any responsibility—*Radical Responsibility*.

What is Radical Responsibility? It's simple to define but far more challenging to live out. It's the act (or maybe the mindset?) of taking

100% ownership of your life—every piece of it, every outcome, every consequence, both good and bad.

Here's the kicker: without taking full ownership of your life and everything that happens in it, you'll never build a strong resilience muscle—if you even have one at all.

Maybe the best way to explain Radical Responsibility is to talk about its opposite (and this is where some feathers might get ruffled).

The opposite of Radical Responsibility is victimhood. And here's the hard truth: **victimhood and Radical Responsibility are 100% mutually exclusive.** You simply cannot have both. The laws of the universe—no matter what you've been taught to believe—demand that you choose *one* or the *other*. There's no middle ground. You don't get to dabble in a little of both.

Radical Responsibility is about freedom. It's about ownership. It's about empowerment. But here's the catch: Radical Responsibility comes at a price. It'll cost you your victimhood. And that's a trade you should make every single time because victimhood, plain and simple, is poison to your soul.

Victimhood's most insidious quality is its ability to make you silently surrender your freedom, ownership, and empowerment—while tricking you into believing you're getting a great deal. It wraps itself in a false sense of comfort and righteousness, convincing you it's the safer, easier choice. And yet, despite being this toxic, victimhood has somehow risen to near-celebrity status. Not just in our society, but arguably across the world today.

If victimhood is so terrible, why is it so widely embraced?

Like most vices, victimhood comes with short-term rewards that feel good in the moment while stealing away long-term virtue. Just try telling someone they're far more empowered than they think—that they're not actually a victim. I promise you, their first reaction won't be gratitude. It's like trying to take a bottle of vodka away from an alcoholic. Most will get pissed off. Some will turn downright hostile.

And here's where it gets funny. Some of you reading this right now are nodding along, fully agreeing with me. But as you read further, some of you—those very same people—won't be nearly as thrilled with what I'm saying. That little flicker of discomfort or irritation you might already be feeling? That's your gut telling you something your brain isn't quite ready to process yet.

If that's you—if you feel offended, or irritated, or even outright mad—I *challenge you* to read this entire chapter. Lean into the discomfort. Sit with it. Especially if you don't want to. You might just need this more than anyone.

There's a lot of appeal to embracing and maintaining victimhood. It's comfortable, it's familiar, and it offers rewards—at least in the short term. But while we're examining its perceived benefits, let's go deeper. Let's take a hard look at what victimhood really is: where it comes from, its hidden toxicity, why so many people cling to it so fiercely, and how society shamelessly sells it to us. We'll also explore how to recognize if you're unwittingly embracing it, and more importantly, how to free yourself from its grip and replace it with the far more empowering mindset of Radical Responsibility.

But before we dive into all of that, it's critical to clarify one thing: **being victimized** is *not* the same as embracing victimhood. Being victimized is not a choice. It's a harsh and unavoidable reality. Nearly everyone on this planet has been—or will be—victimized in some form during their life. When you're victimized, it's a legitimate problem, and it often requires some kind of justice or resolution. That's not what we're talking about here.

What we *are* talking about is what happens next. The mindset you choose after the fact. Whether you claim ownership of your life or stay stuck in the comfort of victimhood. That's where the real challenge—and the real power—lies.

However, **"being a victim"** is something entirely different. Unlike being victimized, **being a victim is a choice**—a mindset you adopt, even when you've legitimately been wronged or hurt. And let me be clear: it's not a good choice.

The parts of your life where you embrace victimhood will, at best, leave you stuck in stagnation—spinning your wheels, unable to move forward. At worst, it will sabotage and completely undermine any efforts to grow, flourish, or create meaningful change. Victimhood keeps you in a self-imposed prison, with no progress, no power, and no way out—unless *you* decide to let it go.

Let's break down the difference between victimization, victimhood, and Radical Responsibility.

If I'm walking down the street, minding my own business, and I get mugged, then I have been **victimized**. The person who mugged me caused harm, plain and simple. However, what happens next is entirely up to me, and I have two choices:

1.) I can choose victimhood. I can see all of humanity as dangerous and untrustworthy. I can stay stuck, pouring my energy into being angry long after the event is over. I can blame others who had nothing to do with my mugging—or society in general—for my misfortune. I can complain that *"somebody"* needs to do something to make the streets safer and convince myself that none of this is my responsibility because, *"I'm a victim, goddammit, and there's nothing I should or can do differently!"* I can decide that people are just evil and let that bitterness eat me alive. I can shout about how anyone who sees this incident differently is "victim shaming" or "victim blaming." And I can wait—*indefinitely*—for someone else to fix the problem, knowing deep down that the only "somebody" who will fix anything is *nobody*.

Or...

2.) I can choose Radical Responsibility. I can take a step back and look at the situation through a lens that is more uncomfortable in the short term but infinitely more empowering in the long run. I can ask myself if walking down that street at that particular time was the wisest decision. I can acknowledge that, while most people are good, there will always be bad apples out there. I can take ownership by deciding to equip myself better for the future—maybe by learning self-defense or arming myself for protection. I can even choose to forgive my attacker—not for their sake, but for *mine*—to release the weight of resentment and move forward with my life.

I could go on and on with this example, but I think you get the point.

Here's the question you have to ask yourself: While one of these two options is clearly more difficult in the near term, requiring uncomfortable self-examination and accountability, **which path looks more desirable in the long run?** Do you want to stay stuck in bitterness and blame, or do you want to reclaim your power, take ownership, and move toward growth and freedom?

Consider the inspiring story of Chris Gardner, whose life journey was immortalized in the movie *The Pursuit of Happyness*. In the early 1980s, Gardner was a struggling salesman living in San Francisco.

His challenges were monumental: a failed relationship, homelessness, and the overwhelming responsibility of raising his young son as a single parent. At times, Gardner and his son slept in shelters, public restrooms, or wherever they could find safety.

In those dark moments, Gardner, like many would, initially felt trapped in a victim mentality. He often thought, *"Why me? Why does life keep throwing these challenges at me?"* This mindset, while completely understandable, left him focused on what he couldn't control, deepening his sense of helplessness and keeping him stuck.

Then came a turning point. One day, Gardner was standing in front of a prestigious brokerage firm when he saw a man step out of a shiny red Ferrari. Unable to ignore his curiosity, Gardner asked, *"What do you do, and how do you do it?"* The man explained that he was a stockbroker. That brief exchange sparked a light inside Gardner. For the first time, he saw a way out—a path to stability and financial security for himself and his son.

This moment didn't change Gardner's circumstances overnight, but it changed his mindset. Instead of asking, *"Why me?"* he began to ask, *"What can I do to change my situation?"* That shift—from helplessness to personal responsibility—was the catalyst for his transformation. Gardner realized that while blaming external circumstances might feel justified, it wouldn't move him forward. If he wanted a better life, he had to create it.

So he did. Gardner applied for a competitive, unpaid internship program at Dean Witter Reynolds, a brokerage firm. He had no financial background, no safety net, and no home—but he had resolve. By day, he immersed himself in learning the complexities of stock trading, while by night, he focused on keeping his son safe and cared for. Gardner's circumstances didn't define him because he refused to let them.

Throughout this grueling period, Gardner faced rejection after rejection, setback after setback. Still, his mindset stayed locked on his vision. He believed, *"I am the captain of my own ship,"* and that belief fueled him through every hardship. Gardner's relentless determination paid off. He earned a full-time position at Dean Witter Reynolds and, years later, founded his own brokerage firm, Gardner Rich & Co. His journey—from homelessness to becoming a multimillionaire businessman and globally recognized motivational speaker—is proof of what happens when you choose Radical Responsibility over victimhood.

Chris Gardner's story reminds us of a critical truth: a victim mentality will keep us stuck in a cycle of blame, helplessness, and stagnation. It may offer a temporary refuge, but it ultimately robs us of our power to create change. Gardner's ability to shift his focus from external circumstances to internal responsibility was the key to his success. His resilience, mental toughness, and positive outlook allowed him to transform his struggles into stepping stones.

The takeaway? Life will knock you down. Hard. But as Chris Gardner proved, you don't have to stay there. Empowerment begins the moment you stop asking *"Why me?"* and start asking *"What can I do to change this?"*

At the very heart of victimhood lies something deeply personal: our morals and core values. If you feel like a victim, it ultimately boils down to one thing—someone or something violated the morals or core values you hold dear. And here's where it gets interesting: this violation doesn't even have to involve you personally (more on that in a minute—and yes, there's an oddly humorous side to this).

Now, don't get me wrong. Morals and core values are generally a *good* thing. They guide our choices, define our character, and help us live with purpose. But it's also important to recognize that both are entirely subjective, shaped by our experiences, upbringing, and beliefs. They're constructs of the human imagination—something we create and hold on to for meaning.

And here's where some of you, particularly those with deeply held religious or spiritual views, might want to jump in and argue with me. I get it. I truly do. So, let me save us both some time: let's agree to disagree if we must. If your point of view works for you—if it brings you peace, purpose, and clarity—*hold on to it*. Don't let me or anyone else tell you otherwise. Fair?

(However—and this is important—if you've picked up this book and read this far, it probably means *something* in your worldview or life isn't working quite the way you want it to. So... let's keep going, shall we?)

To illustrate my point about morals and core values, let's look at something universally regarded as the most evil act one human can commit against another: murder. Animals kill each other all the time, and no one passes moral judgment on it. We don't call it evil; we call it *"the circle of life."*

In fact, animals do all kinds of things we'd consider horrific if humans did them: they kill, they steal, they bully, they discriminate, they even rape. And aside from a handful of exceptions, we don't lose sleep over it. We don't scream about injustice or demand justice when it happens in the animal kingdom. We shrug it off as *"Mother Nature doing her thing."*

Here's the takeaway: the very concept of victimization—and even more so, victimhood—is a creation of the human mind. It exists only because of the moral and value systems we've invented for ourselves. And no, this isn't just playing semantics. This distinction is critical if you genuinely want to break free from victimhood and step into empowerment.

Understanding that victimhood isn't some natural law, but rather a product of the stories we tell ourselves, can be the first step toward reclaiming your power.

On that note, let's ask the question that should be glaringly obvious at this point: If victimhood is so harmful and toxic, why do people cling to it so fiercely and refuse to let it go? The answer is simple. The benefits of victimhood are damn near irresistible.

When you're a victim, nothing is ever your fault. When you're a victim, you get to claim moral superiority. When you're a victim, the world should be kinder to you. When you're a victim, nobody holds you accountable. Victimhood provides the ultimate platform for virtue signaling. It garners heaps of sympathy and makes people rally to your defense, no matter what you do.

When you're a victim, others are the ones who need to change, not you. And let's be real—this also makes victimhood the greatest labor-saving device ever invented. Why do the hard work of self-reflection and growth when you can simply place the blame elsewhere?

So, at the end of the day, victimhood comes down to a single transaction: as the victim, you get to claim superiority. But in return, you give up your power. It's really that simple. You get the illusion of control, but in reality, you're trading your own agency for the comfort of feeling justified.

Mark Manson had one of the most powerful, yet humorous ways of describing this in his book, *The Subtle Art of Not Giving a F*ck*. He introduced the concept of "victimhood chic," which is an insightful take on how people seem to flaunt their victimhood as a kind of badge of honor. But Manson didn't stop there. He took it a step further by introducing the idea of "victimhood by proxy" — a concept that really drives home the lengths people will go to in order to claim or hold on to their victimhood status.

So how does victimhood by proxy work? Well, if we can't find our own victimhood to cling to, we'll gladly latch on to someone else's. We do this by supposedly supporting the victim — and in doing so, we get to feel like we're victims ourselves. This happens when Person A, who isn't a victim at all, gets offended on behalf of Person B (or a group of people) who claims to be victimized, and often is stuck in or choosing victimhood. It's a curious way to gain some moral high ground without actually having to experience any real adversity yourself.

Something that I find particularly interesting is the number of people who genuinely believe they're embracing Radical Responsibility and empowerment, yet are actually living in victimhood without even realizing it. The telltale sign of this is often found in their own words. If you catch yourself, or anyone else, expressing blame, anger or offense—toward anyone, anything, or even themselves— for any reason, that's almost always a clear indication that victimhood is creeping through. It's a subtle but powerful giveaway that the person may be clinging to the very thing they're trying to escape.

A non-exhaustive list of other words and phrases that illustrate victimhood status leaking out (but certainly aren't limited to) includes: "It's not fair," "It's not my fault," "I can't help it," "Nothing I can do," "Someone or something is against me," "I have no choice," "I'm not good enough," "Others have it easier (or have 'privilege' others don't have)"… and the list goes on. While we are all human and everyone experiences negative emotions from time to time, when we find ourselves living in those emotions—especially anger—there's a very high likelihood that it's not just a fleeting feeling, but victimhood itself at work. It's a subtle, but powerful force that can easily be mistaken for just another part of the human experience.

Victimhood is such a powerful and addictive force that many well-established institutions in our society—and in the world—use it as a cornerstone.

Our political system (and I'm talking every side of the aisle here) is 100% dependent on convincing every subset of the population that they are either victims or at risk of becoming victims, and that they need to vote for whoever promises to save and protect them from the "boogeyman du jour." Show me a politician who advocates for people putting on their big boy or big girl panties, taking ownership of their problems and solutions, and I'll show you the loser of that election John F. Kennedy would be politically annihilated these days for saying, "Ask not what your country can do for you. Ask what you can do for your country."

Politics does such an effective job of convincing us all that we're victims of one kind or another that they've effectively got half of the country believing that the other half is completely made up of people who are stupid and evil. Yet, every one of those "stupid and evil" people is 100% convinced that everyone who thinks they're stupid and evil is, indeed, STUPID AND EVIL. Point this out, and you'll rarely find anyone who disagrees with the folly of it all. Then, in their very next breath, they'll almost always "yahbut" into saying it's all because those on the other side are...STUPID AND EVIL.

Organized religion is also heavily fueled by victimhood. Nearly all of them claim persecution and discrimination at some point or another. And when they are actually targeted, they rarely take ownership of their own contribution to said persecution.

In fact, when you think about it, a significant portion of our economy runs on victimhood. And if I really wanted to peel back the layers of the onion (which would make for one long-ass chapter), victimhood creeps into damn near every part of our lives, in some way or another.

But, besides my shooting darts at it for several pages, is it really that important to vigilantly rid our lives of something that's so intertwined with all we've always held dear, helps us make sense of the world—and feels so good & saves us so much unnecessary work? Well, shit, this is a book on resilience, positive mindset, mental toughness, and helping people transform themselves into knowing that **YOU CAN DEAL WITH ANYTHING**, so yes. But then, I felt the need to back up this claim.

So I have a study

This article, which was peer-reviewed—so I'm considering it a study—from PositivePsychology.com explores the concept of a victim mentality and its implications for resilience and self-efficacy. A victim mentality (as articulated by this study—I've already shared my own characteristics of victim mentality) is defined by a persistent belief that one is powerless and that external circumstances dictate their life outcomes. People with this mindset often feel trapped, blame others or external events for their problems, and struggle to take constructive action. The victim mentality is closely tied to an external locus of control, where individuals attribute success or failure to outside forces rather than their own actions. This mindset inhibits growth and perpetuates feelings of helplessness. By fostering an internal locus of control, individuals learn to see themselves as active agents in their lives, which builds resilience and self-efficacy.

Taking personal responsibility for one's choices and circumstances is a cornerstone of overcoming victimhood. Responsibility doesn't mean self-blame (in fact, I believe "self-blame" is just another form of blame, and thus, another form of victimhood); instead, it involves recognizing one's capacity to respond to and influence situations. Responsibility empowers individuals to act in ways that align with their values and goals, even when faced with adversity.

Resilience is developed by confronting challenges, reframing setbacks as opportunities for growth, and seeking solutions rather than dwelling on problems. Key strategies include cognitive restructuring (changing how one interprets events), mindfulness practices, and goal setting.

Self-efficacy, or the belief in one's ability to influence outcomes, plays a crucial role in overcoming a victim mentality. Developing small, achievable goals helps individuals experience success and gradually builds confidence in their capabilities.

So, the study showed that overcoming a victim mentality requires shifting from an external to an internal locus of control, embracing personal responsibility, and building self-efficacy. These changes promote resilience by empowering individuals to take constructive action, reframe challenges, and persist in the face of adversity. The article's points are strongly supported by psychological research, emphasizing the transformative power of responsibility and agency in fostering mental toughness. (https://positivepsychology.com/victim-mentality/?)

Putting Down a Concrete, Day-to-Day How

Now that I've spent a whole bunch of paper and ink (and with some help from the study above) hopefully dismantling the comfort of victimhood, let's talk about how to make the mental shift from victimhood to Radical Responsibility. And once again, the study did some of the heavy lifting for me.

It's a three-step mental process, and it's incredibly simple:

1. **Look at every significant or major event in your life as neither good nor bad.** Intentionally view these events as neutral (hint: they really are).

2. **Take full ownership of the situation. Take full ownership of the solution. And take full ownership of the outcome.** This means that, good or bad, the situation is yours. Regardless of your role in creating the situation, even if you had no role at all in its creation, you own it. Every last drop of it. This is not to say that, when someone is *truly* victimized, justice becomes less important. It means that, even in those situations, we take full responsibility for all of it.

3. **Add an overarching meaning to the situation that empowers you and eliminates any meaning tied to victimhood.** Train yourself to see the opportunities and lessons that exist within every situation.

By following these steps, you're not just shifting your mindset; you're stepping into the power of ownership, embracing the responsibility that transforms adversity into fuel for growth.

So, in 2016, I found myself standing at one of the major crossroads in my life. My wife of nearly three decades was done with me and wanted a divorce. When I broke the news to one of my best friends, his immediate response was, "You made this happen." That comment hit me like a kick to the gut in that moment, yet deep down, I knew he was absolutely right. I had put her through a lot over the years and contributed very little in return. No excuses.

I was beyond pissed off about the fraud lawsuit I was forced to defend myself against. I had no way to get justice or prove that the plaintiff actually knew the lawsuit was frivolous, which it was—and I'll go to my grave believing they knew it was frivolous. At the time, I was working under the full legal and compliance umbrella of two major players in the financial and insurance industries, selling a financial product they had vetted and approved with their vast resources. They practically begged me to sell these welfare benefit trusts, yet when the lawsuit came down, they refused to help me in any way. It felt like the most unfair thing I had ever experienced!

But I also knew that this product and concept were an aggressive use of tax laws, and there would be risk associated with it (which, once again, I fully disclosed). And I chose to take that risk. My clients were getting a huge tax benefit, and I was getting a hefty paycheck in the deal both of which clouded our judgment At the end of the day, I made a choice, and it backfired on me.

I was teetering on the edge of becoming a "bitter old man," consumed by anger toward all the people I felt had wronged me. It seemed like I was heading down a path where resentment would be my only companion. And then, right at that moment, the opportunity for the cross-country bike adventure came into my life. No question, it was a chance for me to metaphorically flip both middle fingers at the world, as if to say, "You're not going to turn me into a bitter old man."

From there, perhaps largely because I was gifted the opportunity to live my greatest dream in such a way that brought me immense praise and recognition, I found myself emotionally unburdened enough to finally realize, for the first time in my life, that I'm not a victim. I've never been a victim. The unfortunate circumstances I found myself in, in a very real way, were freeing me to live this dream.

Since 2016, and especially since August 2022, the simple Radical Responsibility formula I mentioned earlier has evolved from something I discovered into a mental habit that I apply in all circumstances. By learning to reframe, especially the negative events in your life, and embracing Radical Responsibility, big challenges become eclipsed by the confident knowledge that **YOU CAN DEAL WITH ANYTHING**!

Chapter 9: Attitude Aerobics

"Be kind whenever possible. It is always possible." -Dalai Lama

I received a text from my younger daughter, Stefani, that absolutely lit up her day—and, honestly, it made my day too! But what was even more remarkable was that it made the day of a nameless stranger, someone neither of us would ever meet.

It was a late morning in April 2016 when I got the text. Stefani was 21 years old at the time, a full-time cosmetology student working at a grocery store, and like most 21-year-olds, struggling to make ends meet. She wasn't living an easy life, but she was making it work. On that particular morning, she texted me to tell me that, on her way to work, she had stopped at the drive-through at a fast-food restaurant right in front of the grocery store. She mentioned that, even though she was broke, she felt compelled to do something she didn't fully understand at the time. She'd heard me talk about the concept of "Attitude Aerobics" before and, out of the blue, decided to pay for the breakfast order of the person in the car behind her.

Afterward, she drove to work, thinking little more about it. But unbeknownst to her, the person she had helped had apparently watched her park and go into work. A couple of hours later, when Stefani came out after her shift, she found a note on her windshield. It was from the man whose breakfast she had paid for, and he thanked her—not just for the meal, but for the thoughtful gesture itself and what it had meant to him. He shared that he'd been going through a tough week, and her small act of kindness had restored his faith in humanity. The note was heartfelt, and it was clear that the gesture had made a profound impact on him.

Stefani was deeply moved when she read it, and I could feel that same sense of emotion when she texted me to tell me about it. What she'd done had touched both of us, and I couldn't help but feel how contagious that kind of kindness really is. It was a simple, yet powerful reminder of how little things can make a world of difference.

BBQing the Sacred Cow of PMA

The concept and title *"Attitude Aerobics"* is something I borrowed from a man named Nick Murray, who introduced it in his book, *"Serious Money"*. The book, primarily written for financial services reps new to the industry, landed in my hands when I was a brand-new financial advisor in the early 1990s.

Murray's *Attitude Aerobics* asserted that few topics get more lip service—especially from parents, teachers, coaches, and sales managers—while remaining so poorly understood, than the idea of *Positive Mental Attitude (PMA)*. As Murray brilliantly points out, *"They all tell you that you need a good attitude in order to accomplish anything, but they never tell you how to get one."* That statement struck me so deeply it's stayed with me ever since and, in part, inspired me to write this very book more than 30 years later (but I digress).

The way most people talk about improving your attitude is ridiculous. It's generally accepted that all you need to do to get a PMA—Positive Mental Attitude—is simply *decide* to have one. By now, you probably already know how much bullshit I think that is. Murray nailed it when he said you can no more *"decide"* to have a better attitude than you can *decide* to become a world-class triathlete after years of sitting on the couch. His awesomely memorable phrase, *"Positive mental attitude is to psychology as voodoo is to neurosurgery,"* still makes me laugh every time I think about it.

Just like getting into better physical shape requires actually behaving differently—moving your body, training consistently—you've got to behave differently if you want to improve your mindset. I know not everyone agrees, but I've found so much truth in that way of thinking.

Murray's *Attitude Aerobics* concept is built on three basic assumptions we can all hold about ourselves and our fellow humans:

1. Nobody is walking around suffering from too much kindness being heaped upon them by the world.
2. Every single person on earth is vitally interested in themselves and wishes everyone else was too.
3. Everything we put out into the universe—whether positive or negative—comes back to us *"in time and in kind."*

Call it karma, or just plain old *"what goes around comes around."* Whatever you call it, the lesson is the same: how you choose to act matters, and it matters a lot.

So, because of these basic truths about humanity, there's incredible power and opportunity in even the simplest acts of kindness and gratitude. It's not just about the impact on others—there's something transformative that happens within *you* when you behave in ways that lift someone else up.

As Nick so wisely puts it, *"You can do a number of genuinely effective things to affect your attitude. And the one thing they all have in common is: they're all things you do for other people."*

Consider the remarkable story of tennis great Andre Agassi. In the early 1990s, Agassi was at the peak of his professional career, yet he was profoundly unhappy. Despite his status as a world champion, his personal life was in turmoil, and he struggled with motivation, feeling trapped in a sport he openly claimed to hate. His public persona radiated confidence, but behind the scenes, he wrestled with self-doubt, disconnection, and a sense of purposelessness. At one point, Agassi's rankings plummeted, and his career looked like it was unraveling. Frustrated and bitter, he was caught up in everything he thought was wrong in his life, falling into a victim mentality that drained his resilience and his love for the game.

Agassi's transformation began with something simple yet profound: an act of kindness. At his lowest point, he started volunteering to help children in need, particularly in education. In 1994, he founded the *Andre Agassi Foundation for Education*, focusing on providing underprivileged kids with access to quality schooling. The foundation later opened the *Andre Agassi College Preparatory Academy* in Las Vegas, giving countless children opportunities they otherwise wouldn't have had.

Through his work with these kids, Agassi began to see life from a different perspective. Witnessing their struggles and triumphs shifted his focus away from his own frustrations and onto the positive impact he could make in their lives. This shift sparked something in him: a renewed sense of purpose. By focusing on others, Agassi cultivated gratitude—for his platform, his talents, and the opportunities he once took for granted. Tennis, which had felt like a burden, became something entirely different: a vehicle for creating change.

Instead of resenting the sport, he reframed it as a way to fuel his foundation and his mission. Agassi realized that by embracing his career, he could amplify his ability to help others. This new mindset gave him something bigger to play for, and it reignited his passion and his drive. He trained harder, with a renewed sense of responsibility— not just for himself, but for the kids his foundation supported.

Agassi's comeback was nothing short of stunning. In the late 1990s, he climbed his way back from being ranked 141st in the world to becoming the oldest player to hold the No. 1 ranking in tennis at age

33. Along the way, he won five more Grand Slam titles, including the French Open, which completed his career Grand Slam. But more importantly, he became a more grounded, fulfilled version of himself. His philanthropic work expanded, providing millions of dollars in aid and opportunities to children.

Agassi's story is a powerful reminder of how acts of kindness and gratitude can transform not only the lives of others but the life of the giver. By shifting his focus from his own struggles to a larger purpose, Agassi unlocked his full potential, building the resilience and mental toughness needed to overcome adversity. His renewed success on the court wasn't just about personal achievement; it was about serving something bigger than himself.

Andre Agassi's journey illustrates a profound truth: when we show up with kindness and gratitude, we don't just lift others—we lift ourselves. We move beyond bitterness, find purpose, and build the kind of resilience that allows us to thrive in the face of life's challenges.

Just a Dab'll Do Ya

My cross-country bicycle journey is, without question, my "granddaddy of examples" here. The fact that I was privileged enough to do something I was already planning to do anyway—but now got to do it as a big act of kindness—is what changed my life. Sure, it cast me in an over-the-top positive light in the eyes of others, and I'll admit, that kind of attention felt pretty good. But the real story lies in how it transformed the perception I had of *myself*.

And that's the magic, isn't it? Kindness has a funny way of not only lifting others but reshaping how we see ourselves. I'd wager that it did the same thing for Andre Agassi. His renewed purpose in helping others gave him a new lens through which to view his life, his career, and his struggles. I experienced something remarkably similar. When you lean into something bigger than yourself, when you show up for others, it has a way of redefining *you*—not just in the eyes of the world but, far more importantly, in your own.

To be able to block out several months of my life and devote myself entirely to such an endeavor was, in itself, a privilege—one not afforded to most people who have jobs, families, and other real-world responsibilities. (And let's be honest, Nick Murray wasn't talking about crazy-ass adventures when he introduced *Attitude Aerobics*.) The same goes for Andre Agassi. Few people have the resources to start an educational foundation or fund the construction of a school. Hell, you don't even need to be the person who pays for someone's breakfast in the drive-thru.

What you *can* do—what anyone can do—is practice a simple discipline: regularly putting your gratitude *on the record*. That's it. Just showing up with intentional, written expressions of appreciation can make you an Attitude Aerobics…*stud*. And by "on the record," I (and Nick) mean putting those thoughts into written form. Nick, for his part, insisted on handwritten thank-you notes. I won't even go that far. He wrote his book in the early 1990s—long before the golden age of social media. Expressing gratitude has never been easier than it is right now.

But if you're wondering how this concept works its *magic*, let's look at the example Nick used in his book.

Imagine you're having lunch at your usual sit-down restaurant. Like always, you're on the receiving end of good service—nothing unusual there. But this time, before you leave, you pull out a business card or even just a napkin and jot down a quick note: *"Hey, I really appreciate your service today. As a professional myself, I notice when someone goes above and beyond, and you did just that. Thank you! – (Your Name)"*. You leave the note on the table alongside your usual tip.

Now imagine yourself as the server who finds that note. Chances are, they're just going through their day like usual, showing up and doing their job—like always. And then, out of nowhere, someone *noticed*. For maybe the first time ever, someone recognized their effort, even in the most minimalist way. There's a near-100% chance that this tiny act of acknowledgment will give that person a small swell of pride and an extra spring in their step—if only for a few minutes.

It costs you nothing. It takes almost no time. Yet it has a disproportionate impact, both on the recipient *and* on you. That's the real magic of Attitude Acrobics.

Now, imagine yourself as the person doing this sort of thing. It costs you a whopping 45 seconds out of your day—maybe the back of a business card to jot down a quick note. And if you really want to get *fancy*, you could write an actual letter, slip it into an envelope, stick on some postage, and send it off. But let's be honest—that's clearly *a lot* of work, and there's a financial investment involved at this point (sarcasm fully intended).

Now, let's take this even further: imagine you commit to doing this *three times a day*. That's it. Just three quick acts of kindness or expressions of gratitude. Soon, you'd start going through your day *looking* for opportunities to brighten someone's moment—even in the smallest way. Maybe it's a server, a cashier, a coworker, or a stranger in passing. Over time, you'll notice something remarkable: you're not just noticing these opportunities—you're expecting and *hoping* for good things to come back **your** way.

And that shift—this subtle rewiring of how you interact with the world and the people in it—will fundamentally change your outlook. As Nick Murray so brilliantly says, *"Gotcha! That's real positive mental attitude!"*

The best part? You're not "deciding" to have a positive mental attitude —you're *behaving* yourself into it. NOW, just try and *not* feel like **YOU CAN DEAL WITH ANYTHING**!

Go ahead, I dare you.

Let's crank it up one more notch and make this "AA Concept" just a teensy bit more high-octane.

As I've alluded to before: *"If you can take a painful or difficult experience you've had and use it as a means to help someone else get through a painful or difficult experience they're having, you turn your own pain into a blessing."*

Those words just kind of fell out of my mouth after about three hours of Rick Lockridge interviewing me in a park in DeFuniak Springs, Florida. It was halfway through my 2016 journey when Facebook somehow caught wind of how I was using their platform for philanthropy. Next thing I knew, they were sending out a videographer to film a short video—something they apparently intended to show at one of their company-wide meetings. That videographer's name was Rick Lockridge.

As part of the process, there were hours of on-camera interviews. After rambling on and on for what felt like an eternity, I finally blurted out that line. I hadn't planned it. I didn't write it. It just came tumbling out. Rick immediately stopped what he was doing, looked at me, and said, *"Now that is a graduate-level soundbite!"* He clearly recognized the weight of what I'd just said.

And yet...my "graduate-level soundbite" ended up on the cutting room floor.

But here's the thing: it doesn't matter. That moment still stands as a challenge to you and me—a challenge to push further on this holy grail of Attitude Aerobics.

The truth is, every last one of us has been through some painful experiences. It's just part of being human. The challenge—and the opportunity—is to use that pain in some way to help others. And if you can find someone going through the *same* struggle you've been through—someone still in the thick of it—you have a chance to turn your pain into something meaningful.

Let's take all the crap life throws at us and turn it into something good. Let's turn it into a blessing.

There IS a Catch To This

This whole idea holds water *only* to the extent that you want and expect absolutely nothing in return from anyone—except for the satisfaction in your own heart and mind that you've done good for your fellow man or woman. If you perform an act of kindness or gratitude with the idea of getting something in return, then, in my best Willy Wonka voice, *"YOU LOSE! GOOD DAY, SIR!"*

If you expect—and I would even say, *hope for*—recognition or reciprocation, it won't just erode the benefits of Attitude Aerobics; it violates the very essence of it. My daughter didn't race to Facebook or Instagram the moment she paid for that man's breakfast to broadcast her good deed to the world. She did share the story and her resulting excitement with me—and with good reason!—but that wasn't *why* she did it, and that distinction is everything.

"Now, wait just a damn minute here, Mark!" you might say. "Didn't your big act of kindness play out entirely on Facebook for the whole world to see? Didn't it result in an abundance of sunshine being blown up your backside? And weren't you on the receiving end of *hella* attention from the media because of all this?"

Yes. Yes. And YES!

And I ain't gonna lie—*all* that attention and validation from every direction felt GRRRREAT!! But here's the thing: I didn't do any of it *for* those reasons. And I think that fact came through loud and clear, which is, at least in part, why I received so much positive attention.

As I said probably 200 times or more during that journey, *"Nobody does anything for purely altruistic reasons. Everyone involved in things like this should benefit in some way."*

My friend Howie Nestel—one of the biggest philanthropists in South Texas, and an extraordinarily successful businessman largely *because* of his never-ending charitable work—puts it this way: *"Doing good should set you up to do well. Just don't make that the reason you do good."*

Let that sink in for a second.

Even small, seemingly insignificant acts of kindness or gratitude add up to something huge over time. And when you do them consistently, and for the right reasons, the way you see *yourself* begins to shift. Your confidence builds. Your optimism grows. You'll reach the point where you know—deep in your bones—that **YOU CAN DEAL WITH ANYTHING***!*

Chapter 10: Supportive Village

"You're only as good as the people who you surround yourself with with" -Marcela Valladolid

Michael Oher, whose life story inspired the movie *"The Blind Side"*, grew up in Memphis, Tennessee, facing unimaginable challenges shaped by poverty, instability, and neglect. His mother battled addiction, and much of Michael's childhood was spent bouncing between foster care, homelessness, and uncertainty. By the time he reached his teenage years, he had attended numerous schools, with little consistency or support in his education. Feeling abandoned and invisible, Michael struggled with self-esteem and a growing sense of hopelessness.

Everything began to change when the Tuohy family entered his life. Leigh Anne and Sean Tuohy, along with their children, didn't just see a troubled kid from a rough background—they saw *Michael*. They recognized his potential and welcomed him into their home, providing not just material stability but something far more valuable: love, belief, and a sense of belonging.

The Tuohys' support went beyond food, shelter, or access to education. They saw Michael as worthy of success and happiness and challenged him to see the same in himself. Leigh Anne and Sean held him accountable, pushing him to take his academics seriously and develop the discipline that would carry over into sports and life. Their faith became a spark that ignited Michael's own belief in his abilities, shifting his focus from what he lacked to what he *could* achieve.

Michael also found encouragement beyond the Tuohys, from teachers, coaches, and members of his community who invested in him. These relationships, combined with his new family's unwavering support, formed a circle of care that helped Michael cultivate resilience, mental toughness, and a more hopeful outlook on life.

With this foundation, Michael began to thrive. He worked tirelessly to improve his grades, eventually earning a football scholarship to the University of Mississippi, where he became a standout player. His hard work and perseverance didn't stop there—Michael went on to play in the NFL, achieving great success as an offensive tackle and even winning a Super Bowl with the Baltimore Ravens.

But beyond the trophies and accolades, Michael Oher's story is one of profound transformation. It's a testament to how the support of family, friends, and mentors can empower someone to break cycles of adversity and build a fulfilling life. In his memoir, *I Beat the Odds*, Michael reflects on how pivotal those relationships were: the people who believed in him when he couldn't yet believe in himself, and who gave him the tools and accountability to grow into the person he was meant to be.

Key Lessons from Michael Oher's Journey:

1. The Power of Support:
A strong support system—whether it's family, friends, or mentors—provides the emotional and practical resources needed to overcome even the toughest challenges.

2. Belief Breeds Resilience:
When others believe in you, that belief becomes contagious. It can inspire you to develop the resilience, discipline, and confidence to believe in yourself.

3. Mental Toughness Is Built in Community:
Supportive relationships lay the groundwork for mental toughness by

offering encouragement, accountability, and a sense of stability when life feels chaotic.

Michael Oher's story proves a powerful truth: resilience, mental toughness, and a positive mindset don't develop in isolation. They are nurtured through connection, belief, and the support of others. No one succeeds alone, and when we choose to lift someone up, we give them the greatest gift of all: the chance to rise.

What strikes me most about Michael's story is how *obvious* it seems—how common sense it is to recognize the value and power of a Supportive Village when we create, identify, and nurture it properly. And yet, for most of my life, I was completely blind to this truth. I wasn't intentional—hell, I was downright *lazy*—about appreciating the wealth of connection I already had. I didn't see the riches of love, support, and encouragement that surrounded me, and I certainly didn't do much to nurture those beautiful relationships.

It wasn't until I told the world about my cancer diagnosis that I got a much-needed slap upside the head. The sheer outpouring of support, kindness, and encouragement was overwhelming—this wave of people reminding me, loud and clear, that I was not alone. That was my wake-up call. With all these amazing people in my corner, I realized something life-changing: **I CAN DEAL WITH ANYTHING***!*

The importance of having a Supportive Village, especially in the context of adversity, was something I hadn't fully grasped until my friend Pavithri Kilgore really hammered it home. It was that crucial pillar of support hiding in plain sight. Pavithri, a law school graduate and human resources consultant who immigrated to the U.S. from Sri Lanka early in life, shared something with me that stuck. She told me that she had never lacked confidence or self-assurance—until she struck out on her own as an entrepreneur. For the first time, she found herself questioning whether she had done enough to build a solid support system.

It was after that conversation with her that everything clicked for me. Having a Supportive Village isn't just important; it's essential. But what matters even more is populating our village with the right people, and nurturing the right kinds of relationships. And we can't forget that maintaining those connections takes effort—it's easy to lose touch, even with the people who matter most.

This isn't something that just happens—it takes intentional work. And honestly, it should be fun. After all, we're talking about friends and family, for godssakes!

Just as I'm sitting down to write this chapter, my phone rings. It's an old friend, Chris Camden, calling to catch up a bit. Chris was a coworker from my financial days, and over the years, we became lifelong friends. Though we lost touch for many years, we reconnected after my cancer diagnosis. He's been one of those incredible voices of encouragement in my life, always expressing how impressed he is with where I am mentally. And that kind of encouragement? It's pure fuel for me to not just meet, but exceed his impression of my mindset!

As busy as he is—he owns and operates a residential painting business—he always makes time to meet me for breakfast regularly, just to keep in touch, talk business, and do a little work together. During our conversation that day, I was updating him on where things stood for me medically.

By this point, I had found out that I was cancer-free, my strength and energy were starting to return, and things were generally looking up.

Chris then began talking with great reverence about a friend of his who had been diagnosed with Hodgkin's lymphoma many years ago and was told he had just six months to live. Yet, this friend is still alive and well, many years later. Chris spoke with awe about everything his friend endured, almost as if his friend and I were both something special—though, to be fair, his friend might just be. As we continued our conversation, it really began to sink in how vital a role people like Chris have played in buoying my mental strength through some really tough times. And the way he was talking about his friend, I could see that Chris had been there for him in much the same way.

I said, "Chris, I need you to understand how crucial it is, when dealing with difficulty like this, to have someone like you encouraging and supporting someone like me. I've never met your friend, the one you were talking about, but I'm absolutely positive that he'd agree with me on this." I continued, "Having a positive mindset is one of the most vital things one can have when dealing with something like cancer. What you're doing—encouraging me—is maybe even more important than all the things the doctors are doing. The role you've played in keeping me positive has been huge! So when you and your other buddy get together, make sure you keep in mind what you've contributed to that."

No matter what you're dealing with, have dealt with, or will deal with, your Supportive Village is going to be the single most important asset you have against adversity. You might be the type of person who isn't very social and seeks every available opportunity to be away from others—and I empathize with that because, as much as I love being around people, I need solitude to recharge. But we are a social species, and we do live in a social world. There's simply no getting around the fact that we all need one another, even if we like to think we don't.

The Common Thread

Of all the points I make in this book about how to create and build a positive mindset for adversity, it's the topic of the immutable value of your people that is most universally agreed upon. Whether it's experienced behavioral health professionals, my oncology team, or just about every leader you talk to on the topics of resilience, positive mindset, and mental toughness, this principle stands as a cornerstone. The importance of having the right people around you—those who support, encourage, and challenge you—cannot be overstated.

When I initially began researching the topic of resilience, I searched for and read dozens of articles, blogs, and watched hours of documentaries from professionals on the "whats and hows" of dealing with challenging circumstances. I can't think of any of these sources that didn't at least mention the value of having a strong human support system. In fact, many of them cited it as the overwhelming, most important factor in resilience. The overall consensus was clear: no matter your circumstances, having the right people around you is the number one key.

I also asked every oncology nurse who got within three feet of me—and believe me, I get within three feet of a lot of oncology nurses—about what they see in their patients who are facing such immense difficulty. When it came to the cancer patients they saw as having the best mindsets, weathering the brutal storms of illness and chemotherapy, and enjoying the best outcomes, every single nurse I spoke with immediately pointed out that having a strong and positive support system was the one common thread these patients shared.

It's not even up for debate.

Think: Give Not Get

Build, identify, and nurture your Supportive Village with the understanding that the people you surround yourself with can make or break you! How you nurture your village is just as important as who you include in it. As the saying goes, "your network is your net worth," but I'm talking about something quite different here.

The expectations you bring into any relationship or friendship will ultimately determine its value and its duration. It doesn't matter what type of relationship we're talking about—business, family, friends, or certainly romantic—you never go into it hoping to get something from it. You enter these relationships with a constant eye on what you bring to the table. What are you contributing to this relationship? Yes, you will ultimately need to get something from it as well—we'll touch on that in a moment. But if you go into any relationship with anything but a giver's heart, don't be shocked when it doesn't turn out the way you envisioned. That is, if it lasts at all.

This reminder is especially pertinent when you're in business or sales and attend networking events. The biggest missed opportunity I see—and sadly, have been guilty of myself—is when people attend these events and play the "short game," thinking purely transactionally. Often under the guise of "helping" people, we approach these events as if they're some sort of Easter Egg Hunt where, behind the faces in the crowd, our rent money for next month is hidden behind one of them, and we just need to find it. These people aren't looking to build potentially valuable long-term relationships. Though I'm poking fun at this behavior, I'm not really judging it. Just keep in mind that these kinds of relationships have very little chance of contributing to your Supportive Village. However, when you network with the goal of creating long-term relationships, where your main focus is giving with no expectation of a contract, order, or commission check, you often end up reaping those very benefits in the long run anyway.

Think: Emotional Bank Account

Every relationship of every kind contains an imaginary bank account. Just like a real bank account, you've got to be able to make withdrawals at some point—otherwise, what's the point? And, also just like a real bank account, in order to make withdrawals, you first have to make deposits. Whenever you see a friendship, business relationship, or romantic relationship go south, there's at least a 95% chance it's because one, or maybe both, of the parties became severely and hopelessly overdrawn in the emotional bank account.

Every act of kindness, gratitude, empathy, loyalty, respect, and love is a deposit into the emotional bank account of that relationship. Conversely, every selfish act, or anything that serves as the opposite of that list, is a withdrawal. The size of the deposit or withdrawal is directly proportional to the magnitude and authenticity of the act that created it. Something to keep in mind here is that this imaginary bank account is not a "fair" system (so, naturally, it mirrors life itself). Withdrawals are far easier to make and tend to be much larger than deposits.

For the love of God, please tell me you already understand that it's possible to spend a lifetime building a relationship, and it takes about five seconds to destroy it.

Think: Fountains and Drains

Obviously, not everyone you bring into your life (or your village) should make it into your inner circle. And not everyone who makes it into your inner circle should get to stay there.

Everyone you've ever known well, and everyone you meet and ultimately come to know well, falls into one of two categories—at least if you adopt my way of thinking: fountains and drains. And this is a two-way street, so you will either be a fountain or a drain to pretty much everyone in your circles, too. Fountains are the people in your life who add something significant enough that you get at least as much from the relationship as you put into it— even if it's a simple friendship. Fountains are the ones you find yourself wanting to be around. They are the ones where you just feel good after every interaction and genuinely look forward to spending more time with them. They may not always be the easiest people to be around, but when that's the case, it's because they hold themselves and you to a high standard in one or more areas of their lives. Drains, on the other hand, are the exact opposite of fountains.

One of the major keys to having the healthiest Supportive Village possible is recognizing which people are your fountains and which are your drains. However, it's just as important to have enough self-awareness to recognize whether you are a fountain or a drain to the people in your circles. You simply keep your fountains closer to you, investing more time and energy with them. You move the drains further away, spending less time and energy with them. You don't necessarily need to cut ties with these people entirely—just move them to your outer circle. No drama, no difficult or awkward conversations needed, although sometimes a "talk" is the healthy, warranted and necessary thing to do. But generally, the best way to handle this is to quietly and gently reduce your attention and presence without fanfare. I'm not talking about "ghosting" people at all, just creating distance.

Sometimes, you'll find someone who is a fountain to you, but you can tell that you're a drain on them. When that happens, treat it just like they are a drain on you and have the courage and grace to gently create space and distance from that person as well.

You really do need a level of courage and confidence—which you should have no shortage of if you're following the Resilience Regimen in full—in order to put this "fountains and drains" principle into practice. Not everyone will understand or approve as you promote or demote the people in your life according to this principle and your heart & gut, but I'm urging you to do so anyway.

Think: Your Five People

You truly are the average of the five people you spend the most time with. Take a moment to look around at your innermost circle—your family, friends, and associates. What are these people like? What do they do? Who do they surround themselves with when they're not with you? What standards do they hold themselves and others to?

You could ask yourself whether these are the people you want to emulate and become like, but nature has a funny way of answering that question for you. If the five people you spend most of your time with are positive, successful, mentally strong, and generous—people who hold themselves to high standards in how they treat themselves and others—chances are, you'll either become the 6th in that group or you'll soon find yourself with a new inner circle. It's simply the nature of how relationships work.

The point here is to always be aware of this reality and to be intentional about it. Reflect on your own core values—or the values you want to adopt, especially if you recognize the need for higher standards—and build relationships with people who share those same values. Then, find ways to be around them as much as possible.

Hold everyone in your village to a high standard, but hold yourself to an even higher one!

Your Village And Vulnerability

A little more than a year ago, I had an interesting conversation with one of my fraternity brothers, Kenny Schnepp. Several of us had recently reconnected after decades of being out of touch. We'd been getting together regularly ever since my cancer diagnosis, and it was amazing how quickly we all slipped back into the friendships we had left behind.

Kenny, whom I would describe as a man of great Christian faith, commented on how incredible—and yet interesting—it was that we had all seemed to pick up right where we left off, despite the fact that most of us hadn't seen one another in over 30 years. He said, "It's weird. Most of our memories and the things we talk about are the stupid party-animal stuff we did back in the day. Yet, after all these years, I find myself at least as close to my fraternity brothers as I am to my brothers in Christ, whom I see every week."

As we continued talking, I think we identified why this was the case. First of all, we were all products of the 1980s, a time when pledging a fraternity was much different than it is today. Back then, "hazing" was a much more significant part of the process. I told Kenny, "There were pledge brothers with whom I had almost nothing in common, but after a semester of cleaning toilets at the fraternity house, doing kitchen duty, or just taking good-natured crap from the active members, it's incredible how close I became with some of these guys."

We further discussed that we were all at the start of our transition into adulthood. Most of us were living away from home, making our own day-to-day decisions for the very first time in our lives. Our futures were now heavily "under construction," and more uncertain than ever. We were all just trying to figure out who we were and what we would become. In a nutshell, it was one of the most vulnerable times in all of our lives.

The point I'm making here is that shared experiences are the single greatest force for creating lasting relationships. And when those relationships are forged in an environment where people are facing vulnerability and/or adversity together, it acts like "quick-setting glue," forging deep relationships very quickly and binding people in a way that tends to last a very long time, if not forever.

Now, take this idea and pair it with the thought that, "if you can take a painful experience you've had and use it as a means of helping someone else with their painful experience, you'll turn your own pain into a blessing." When you put these two ideas together—shared vulnerability, shared pain, and turning it into blessings—it can serve as a powerful roadmap for how to best navigate the process of identifying, building, and nurturing your Supportive Village.

None of this means you need to have an enormous circle of friends and family. It simply means surrounding yourself with a group of people who genuinely love you for who you are, and whom you love for who they are. These are the people who would drop everything to help a friend in need, and you would do the same for them. And, importantly, nobody does any of this with the expectation of receiving anything in return—other than the internal satisfaction of helping a friend in need.

With your Supportive Village in your corner, **YOU CAN DEAL WITH ANYTHING**!

Chapter 11: Healing Humor

"To truly laugh, you must be able to take your pain and play with it." -Charley Chaplin

In 2012, Tig Notaro faced an almost unthinkable cascade of personal and physical challenges. In a matter of months, she battled a life-threatening bacterial infection, endured the sudden death of her mother, went through a painful breakup, and was ultimately diagnosed with breast cancer. By the time the diagnosis came, the weight of it all felt crushing.

Just days later, Notaro was scheduled to perform a stand-up comedy show at the Largo in Los Angeles. Canceling seemed like the obvious choice, but instead, she made the bold decision to take the stage. Rather than deliver a polished routine, she opened her set with the now-famous line:
"Hello. I have cancer. How are you?"

The audience laughed, nervously at first, unsure of how to react. But what followed was nothing short of groundbreaking. Notaro delivered a raw, heartfelt, and wickedly funny account of her struggles—a perfect blend of vulnerability and wit. She didn't shy away from the gravity of her situation, but instead leaned into the absurdity of it all. She joked about the sheer unluckiness of her recent misfortunes, transforming her pain into a shared experience that struck a profound chord with her audience.

By using humor to confront her diagnosis and everything else she'd endured, Notaro reclaimed her narrative. She refused to be defined solely by her circumstances, choosing instead to shape how she experienced and shared them. Her comedy turned her pain into connection, creating a sense of solidarity with her audience. People didn't just laugh; they felt seen. Notaro showed them that humor and heartache could coexist—and that laughter could be healing.

For Notaro, humor also offered a shift in perspective. Finding comedy in her struggles allowed her to defuse some of the fear and sadness she was carrying. Performing that night wasn't just about making others laugh; it was an act of catharsis. Sharing her story helped her process her emotions and release some of the tension that had built up.

Her performance at Largo became legendary. When the set was released as the live album *Tig Notaro: Live*, it went viral, earning widespread acclaim and launching her career to new heights. But more than professional success, that night marked a turning point in Notaro's personal journey. With the same humor and resilience she displayed on stage, she faced her cancer head-on. She underwent a double mastectomy, and by the end of 2012, she was declared cancer-free.

Tig Notaro's story is a testament to the power of humor as a lifeline in the face of adversity. By confronting her challenges with wit and grace, she didn't just survive—she thrived. Her struggles became a source of strength, connection, and inspiration for millions. She reminds us that even in the darkest moments, laughter has the power to illuminate the path forward.

It's no secret that laughter is the best medicine. But let me tell you, writing a chapter about *Healing Humor* and actually trying to be funny while doing it? That's a whole other level of challenge. Humor has always come naturally to me—it's just how I was raised and how I'm wired. It's been my default setting, my go-to survival mechanism.

But as I sit here writing, I can't ignore the fact that not everyone sees the world through the same lens of humor that I do. Some people reading this might not have grown up in an environment where jokes were the family currency or where laughter was the default reaction to adversity. Maybe humor doesn't come as naturally to them, and that's okay.

Recognizing this makes it a challenge for me to explain the value of humor in healing without sounding like I'm saying, "Just be funny, it's easy!" when I know for many, it isn't. Humor is personal, and what works for one person might not resonate with another. It's a skill, a mindset, and sometimes a leap of faith. And that's what makes this topic both important to discuss and tricky to communicate effectively.

The truth is, humor is serious business when it comes to resilience. Honestly, I could write an entire book on this topic alone! But let's face it—while humor is undoubtedly a skill, just like the other four pillars of the Resilience Regimen, by the time you're reading this, your personality is probably cemented enough that you either already "get it" or you don't. And if you don't, well, no chapter is likely to flip that switch completely.

Here's what I want you to take away: I'm not a comedic or behavioral health expert, not even close. But I wholeheartedly believe that if I can laugh at myself through some of the most challenging and literally life-threatening situations imaginable, *anyone* can find the humor in most of the problems they face. Especially the day-to-day nonsense. Seriously, if you can't chuckle at the absurdity of life's little dramas, what's the alternative? Sometimes, laughter is the only thing that keeps us moving forward.

Nothing in the world tickles your Healing Humor bone quite like the science behind it.

The study *"Eustress of Humor Associated with Laughter Modulates Immune System Components: Reduction in Stress Hormones,"* conducted by Dr. Lee Berk and colleagues, highlights the incredible power of laughter to reduce stress and improve overall health. Stress, as we know, raises cortisol levels, weakens the immune system, and leaves us more vulnerable to illness. Dr. Berk's team set out to explore whether humor and laughter could act as natural counterbalances to these harmful effects. Spoiler alert: they absolutely can.

To test their theory, participants were divided into two groups. One group watched a 60-minute comedy video specifically designed to make them laugh, while the other group engaged in neutral activities, like reading (and presumably not laughing). Blood samples were collected throughout the study to measure stress hormones—like cortisol and epinephrine—and immune system markers, such as natural killer (NK) cell activity and immunoglobulin levels, which play a critical role in fighting infections.

The results? Nothing short of amazing. The laughter group saw their cortisol levels plummet by up to 39%, while their immune systems received a noticeable boost. NK cell activity increased, and levels of protective antibodies rose. Beyond the numbers, participants in the laughter group reported feeling happier and more relaxed. In short, humor didn't just help their physical health; it significantly improved their emotional well-being too.

One particularly fascinating concept highlighted in the study is *eustress,* or positive stress. Unlike harmful, chronic stress, eustress activates the body in a way that promotes resilience without causing damage. Laughter creates this beneficial stress, essentially giving your mind and body a gentle workout that leaves you stronger and better equipped to handle adversity.

These findings align with a growing body of research demonstrating that humor is a powerful tool for resilience. Studies have shown that humor not only reduces physical symptoms of stress but also enhances emotional regulation and can even speed up recovery from illness. The practical takeaway? Make laughter a regular part of your life. Whether it's through a hilarious movie, a comedy show, or just swapping goofy stories with friends, laughter is one of the simplest, most enjoyable ways to strengthen your mental and physical health.

Honestly, though, given my relentless sense of humor, how I managed to get so sick in the first place is still a mystery for the scientific community to solve. Maybe I'm just *too* funny for my own good. (Journal of Behavioral Medicine, Berk, L. S., et al. (2001). Eustress of humor associated with laughter modulates immune system components: Reduction in stress hormones.)

In the spring of 2016, during the early stages of my divorce, I found myself completely disoriented and in shock over the whole situation. It felt like my world had been flipped upside down, and I didn't have the first clue how to process it. So, I made one of the smartest decisions I could've at the time: I sought out the help of a therapist.

Physically, I was what I'd describe as being in "messy overdrive." The stress was off the charts—I wasn't sleeping, my mouth felt like sandpaper, I couldn't eat, and I was on edge in ways I'd never experienced before. Every nerve felt frayed.

Maybe 10 minutes into my very first therapy session, the therapist made an interesting observation: she noticed right away that I was using humor as a way of dealing with the heavy stress I was under. I hadn't even realized it, but there I was, cracking joke after joke about my situation—about the divorce, the chaos, everything.

When she pointed it out, my first thought was, *Oh, great. She's about to tell me to stop joking around and be more serious about all of this.* After all, wasn't that what therapists did? Help you dive into the *serious* stuff?

But instead, she surprised me. She said something along the lines of, "You clearly use humor to cope, and that's actually a very healthy mechanism." She didn't just acknowledge it—she encouraged it. That moment was like a permission slip to keep doing what came naturally to me, even in the midst of all the pain and uncertainty.

Looking back, I think her insight was one of the most important takeaways from that first session. Humor wasn't a way of avoiding my feelings; it was how I navigated them. It became both a shield and a lifeline—protecting me just enough to keep moving forward while also letting me process everything in my own way.

Even the U.S. Navy SEAL Teams—the most elite special operations force on the planet—embrace the power of humor. These warriors often find themselves in high-stress, incredibly dangerous, and physically and mentally brutal conditions, living on the edge of death for weeks at a time. And yet, even in these extreme environments, they rely on laughter as a critical tool for resilience.

In a January 2024 article titled **"A Navy SEAL Explains 8 Sources of Grit and Resilience"** by Eric Barker, the 8th source of resilience listed is "Find a Way to Laugh." The article quotes a SEAL who emphasizes just how important humor is, even in the toughest situations:

"You've got to have fun and be able to laugh; laugh at yourself and laugh at what you're doing. My best friend and I laughed our way through BUD/S. We still tell the same jokes whenever I talk to him. It's one of my best memories of going through BUD/S. There's something about when you're facing a really crummy situation, to look over at your friend and see him smile. It tells you, 'Alright, I'm going to be fine. We're going to be fine, and it's all going to work out.'"

Think about that for a second. These are men training and fighting in some of the harshest, most life-threatening conditions imaginable, and yet one of their most powerful tools isn't a weapon or a piece of advanced technology—it's the ability to laugh. To find humor even in the middle of hell on earth.

It's not about ignoring the seriousness of their situation; it's about creating a sense of connection, hope, and perspective. Humor becomes a way to say, *This sucks, but we're still here, and we're going to make it through.* That mindset, that ability to find levity in the darkest of times, is something we can all learn from, no matter what battles we're facing in life.

In the weeks following my diagnosis, my fraternity brother Bob and I spent a lot of time cracking jokes about my cancer situation. Humor was our coping mechanism, and nothing was off-limits. One of our running gags was the idea of creating a spreadsheet ranking which of our fraternity brothers had the highest odds of being the first to die. Unsurprisingly, I was always at the top of the list.

Shortly after my diagnosis, a group of us reconnected for a golf reunion—an event that has since become an annual tradition. Almost immediately (thanks largely to Bob), we started referring to the event as the **"Mark Light Memorial Golf Reunion."** The jokes about my health were relentless and completely inappropriate by most people's standards, but for us, they were pure gold.

At one point, we even considered having Bob dress up in a Grim Reaper costume and show up at the car dealership where I was working part-time. The plan was for him to silently walk onto the showroom floor, approach my desk, and just stand there ominously for several minutes while I pretended not to notice. We laughed ourselves silly every time we talked about this stunt. The dealership's management even signed off on the idea—probably because they didn't believe we'd actually go through with it.

In the end, we decided against it. While it was an absolute riot to us, we realized it might not land so well with others. What we found hysterical might have been deeply unsettling, even offensive, to bystanders. That didn't stop us from laughing about it every time we revisited the idea, though. To this day, those memories remind me how humor helped me keep things in perspective when life felt completely overwhelming.

When using healing humor, it's important to take other people's feelings into account. Sensitivity matters. But beyond that, don't shy away from being a little inappropriate—if the situation calls for it and the audience is right. Ask any medical professional or first responder, and they'll tell you the same thing: to cope with the daily dose of trauma they face, humor is their number one tool. And more often than not, that humor crosses the line into territory most people would consider wildly inappropriate.

The thing is, when you're navigating life-and-death situations—or even just the chaos of daily struggles—sometimes the only way to lighten the load is to find laughter in the darkest, most absurd places. It's not about being disrespectful; it's about survival. For those in high-stakes roles, inappropriate humor can serve as a pressure valve, releasing the unbearable weight of what they see and endure. And maybe, just maybe, the same approach can work for all of us when life throws its own brand of chaos our way.

Now, think about a day in the life of someone in business, sales, or sales leadership. You're constantly dealing with rejection and disappointment—it stings! At times, it can feel like death by a thousand paper cuts. But maybe the best way to handle it, while staying relentlessly focused on the job, is to laugh your ass off at all of it. Find a coworker who can be your "humor partner" in this. Share the absurdity, the frustration, and the downright ridiculousness of the daily grind, and turn it into something you can laugh about together.

As tough and painful as those rejections and disappointments feel in the moment, give it time—usually not even that much time—and they'll transform into some of your fondest memories and favorite stories to tell. During my time as a sales trainer, these war stories of getting my teeth kicked in became incredibly valuable. Not only did they help me illustrate key points and principles, but they also created a bond with my students. They found entertainment in my tales of mishaps and misfires, sure, but more importantly, those stories were proof that I truly understood the struggles they faced in the field. I'd been there. I'd lived it. And somehow, I'd survived—with a sense of humor intact. That connection, born of shared challenges and a willingness to laugh through the pain, became one of the most powerful tools I had in helping others persevere.

One of my favorite memories—and a story I've shared countless times—revolves around "Bertha," a public school principal in Indianapolis. Back in 1995, I was working with her to develop a late-career retirement plan. We met a couple of times to discuss her goals and how I could help, and eventually, we agreed that I'd create a proposal for her. Part of that plan involved her transferring her financial assets for me to manage.

I poured hours into crafting the plan, meticulously dotting every "I" and crossing every "T." When I returned to her school to present it, everything seemed to be going great. We had built what I thought was a strong professional relationship, and I felt confident she'd see the value in what I'd put together. Besides, this plan wasn't just good for her; it was going to be a major boost for my business at a time when I desperately needed every win I could get.

As I wrapped up my presentation, Bertha smiled and said, "Let's go for it." Music to my ears! She was all in, and I was thrilled. Of course, I kept my best poker face to mask the inner celebration going on in my head. As I pulled out the paperwork to finalize everything, she glanced at the stack of forms and asked how long it would take. "Fifteen, maybe twenty minutes," I replied. She hesitated and said, "I've got a meeting to get to. Can we handle the paperwork in a couple of days when I have more time?"

No problem. We set a follow-up meeting at her office. Easy enough—or so I thought.

When I arrived a few days later, Bertha was nowhere to be found. She wasn't in her office, and no one in the building seemed to know where she was. I followed up with a voicemail. No response. I called again. And again. Nothing. I even showed up unannounced at her office, hoping to catch her. Still nothing. Bertha was ghosting me, and I was frustrated beyond belief.

Did she not understand how much time and effort I had poured into this? How could she do me like this after everything I'd done to help her?

The truth is, I'd made some mistakes in my sales process that contributed to the situation, but that's a topic for a different book on a different day. At the time, though, I wasn't reflecting on my errors—I was stewing. Finally, out of sheer frustration, I sat down with a piece of company letterhead and decided to write her a letter.

It started innocently enough: "Dear Bertha." But then I unleashed. The first paragraph consisted entirely of the word "WHY" repeated over and over: "WHY WHY WHY WHY WHY WHY WHY WHY WHY…" I filled the entire paragraph with it, then started another paragraph that was basically the same thing but ended with,

"…..WHY would you do me like this after all the work I've done for you???" And then, in my infinite wisdom, I sent it.

To this day, I can't believe my manager approved that letter.

Bertha never replied, and I never saw or heard from her again. At the time, I wasn't exactly laughing about the situation—but it didn't take long before I was. Before I knew it, I was sharing the story with everyone in my office, and it quickly became one of my go-to tales as a sales trainer. It was perfect for breaking the ice or demonstrating the highs and lows of the profession. Plus, it was a great reminder: sometimes, you just have to laugh at yourself, even when you're getting your teeth kicked in. And trust me, those stories of failure often become some of your best memories—and your best lessons.

Building the skill of Healing Humor boils down to four key principles:

1. **Avoid using humor when you're feeling really low.** If you're at a severe emotional low, attempts at Healing Humor are likely to fall flat or, worse, backfire. Instead of forcing it, give yourself some time to let the emotional dip subside. Humor works best when you're not too deep in the hole.

2. **Remember that humor is both difficult and subjective.** Don't try to be a comedian if you're not one. The goal isn't to get up on stage or tell the perfect joke; it's to find humor in your own life and in the problems you face. Humor, when shared, can amplify the experience and make it even more powerful. And let's be real—nothing draws people to you like a good laugh. This is especially true when humor is woven into *Tactical Vulnerability*, as Tig Notaro demonstrated in her story at the beginning of this chapter. Just keep in mind:

sometimes humor falls flat, and it can make things awkward, or worse, leave you feeling even worse than before.

3. **Always laugh at yourself first.** Using humor as a tool for resilience isn't an excuse to tear others down. Poking fun at yourself and making yourself the butt of your own jokes is a sign of a healthy self-image, and it works wonders for diffusing tension in awkward or painful situations. Plus, it helps you come across as likable and trustworthy. People are drawn to those who can laugh at themselves. However, be cautious—overdoing it can have the opposite effect. I can't pinpoint the exact line, but trust me, it's there, so proceed with care.

4. **Understand where and how to find humor.** The good news is, since we're talking about resilience and dealing with adversity, there's literally no better place to find humor than in the very problems that have caused you pain and heartache. As David Lee Roth, former lead singer of Van Halen, once said, *"Can you think of a time when everything went exactly perfectly and according to plan, but was hilariously funny anyway? Take your time, because I can't."*

No matter how great or terrible your situation may seem, humor is one of the most powerful tools not only for managing difficulty but also for building a *Supportive Village*. Just remember, don't start thinking you're Ricky Gervais at the Golden Globes unless you're looking for even more trouble.

People are naturally drawn to humor—and to those who know how to use it properly. The truth is, no one will ever laugh with you and dislike you at the same time. As humans, we instinctively view those who use humor effectively as more intelligent, more trustworthy, and more approachable. When humor is woven into any aspect of *Tactical*

Vulnerability or your *Supportive Village*, Healing Humor has the power to significantly amplify your efforts and make those efforts feel more connected.

In fact, one could argue that Healing Humor is the glue that holds all the other pillars of the *Resilience Regimen* together. While you're at it, don't lose sight of Healing Humor's actual *physical healing* power! And here's the best part: when it comes to humor, you don't need to be a comedian. You don't need to be the funniest person in the room. All you need is the ability to see a bit of humor in most things—and the courage to use it. When you do, Healing Humor helps you realize something powerful: **YOU CAN DEAL WITH ANYTHING!**

Chapter 12: Conclusion

"The greatest glory in living lies not in never falling, but in rising every time we fall" -Nelson Mandela

One thing I've learned in my nearly six decades on this earth is that painful, difficult, and adverse situations are completely inevitable. These experiences bring with them a power that's directly proportional to the size and scope of the adversity itself.

A rejected cold call, a botched presentation, a lost sale, a commission chargeback, or a lost job—all of these carry with them anything from a small sting to a big kick in the gut for someone making their living in sales. Then, there are the bigger setbacks: the loss of a loved one or a relationship, major legal problems, the collapse of your business, or a serious illness. These kinds of things can, and often do, shake you to your core. They can derail you and damage your psyche in ways both subtle and profound. This was certainly the case for me for most of my life. And much of that damage works in ways that are hard to see, but are very real.

However, those negative experiences can also lead you to some of the most beautiful parts of the human experience. Every difficulty brings with it a choice: You can either see it as something simply bad, which makes you a victim—but a comfortable one. Or, you can view it as an opportunity.

If sales or entrepreneurship is your chosen profession, then you are a risk-taker. Adversity is not only inevitable; it's likely a daily part of your life. The ability to not just weather life's storms and get through problems but to actually learn, grow, and become better as a result is what truly sets you apart. Every bad thing that happens in your world has the power to become the most beautiful part of your life.

One key to making this happen is to be intentional about creating resilience—unlike the way I learned it. The time to build your shelter is when the sun is shining. If you're anything like me, you've probably been executing parts of the Resilience Regimen your entire life.

Confidence in your own resilience is a huge factor in weathering the storm while it's still raging.

I'm reminded of this as I type this very conclusion—barely 40 days after being told I'm cancer-free and just a week after Hurricane Helene unleashed its devastating fury. The need for resilience, a positive mindset, and mental toughness is often greatest, not during the storm, but right after, when it seems like the sun has just come back out and the sky is blue again. This is when the difficult task of "cleanup" begins.

Being resilient, having a positive mindset, and having mental toughness DOES NOT mean always feeling "up" or positive. In fact, it doesn't have much to do with feelings at all. And it doesn't mean everything will magically work out the way you hope—or even work out well at all. Having resilience, a positive mindset, and mental toughness means having the skills, knowledge, habits, and "people resources" sufficient that, no matter how things end up, YOU KNOW, without a doubt, that **YOU CAN DEAL WITH ANYTHING!**

Recap, anyone?

A Couple of Principles to Keep in Mind: This book focuses entirely on mindset. However, resilience will always be a "mind, body, spirit" thing, so don't neglect the other two legs of that stool!

The Resilience Regimen operates using the BE-DO-HAVE model as one of its foundational principles. But it does so with a lowercase "do," which leads the way in the form of behaviors that get you into the BE-DO-HAVE game.

Crafting Your Unshakable Foundation: As important as setting goals is, it's a waste of time if you simply set them and do nothing. As James Clear said, "Your results will never rise to the level of your goals. They will fall to the level of your systems."

The greatest antidote to adversity of any kind is action. Learn from Mark Messner: your odds of good things happening for you are directly proportional to how much you keep your feet moving. And taking action can, and often does, lead you to different and better destinations than you even set out for in the first place!

All waters become much easier to navigate in life when you have a clear purpose that aligns with your core values. You're going to be dead for a longer period of time than you will be alive, so figure out exactly how you want to be remembered, and then live up to that image every day of your life.

("T.R.A.S.H.") Your Daily Dose of Resilience:

Asking for help is a virtue, not a vice. Just make sure you do it right. Uncomfortable and difficult circumstances offer the very best opportunities for growth. So, be intentional about embracing them. Your challenges and the discomfort of staying out of your comfort zone will be some of the most powerful learning experiences you can have—and they can set you up for great things.

You absolutely must take full ownership of your life and everything in it, both the good and the bad. This must be true, no matter what happens. The price of doing so is giving up the relative short-term comfort of victimhood.

A regular habit of selflessly serving others through acts of kindness and gratitude will fundamentally change how you interact with the world. It shifts both the way the world perceives you and how you perceive yourself. Just be sure you never perform these acts with the expectation that they'll be repaid, reciprocated, or even recognized. The true power lies in who you become in your own mind.

The people you surround yourself with are likely the single most important factor in your life. Be very wise about who you allow into your circles, and be even more thoughtful about the type of person you are and what you bring to the lives of the people around you.

Remember, humor makes everything in life better—especially the difficult and painful things. Learn to see humor and use it for its therapeutic benefits. Recognize that everything that goes wrong carries a silver lining, and often, that silver lining is a bit of humor waiting to be found.

Now, to summarize the summary: get the focus off yourself and your own problems! Be a giver, not a taker! And never forget that being valuable is far more fruitful than simply being happy.

Once you've taken the principles outlined in this book and implemented the pillars of the Resilience Regimen, your life will still be your life—and it will not be perfect. In fact, you'll still have problems. It's very likely you'll face big problems, and many of them. And worse, eventually, you'll die just like the rest of us. But at the very least, you'll have acquired a set of skills that will make life a little easier at times. You'll have tools to smooth out the rough edges just a bit.

But at best, you could be like me. I learned these skills and principles over a lifetime—and I did so unknowingly. The accumulation of these skills, along with the life experiences I've had, hasn't necessarily made my life events easier. However, I've experienced a total transformation in my mindset over the last couple of decades. It wouldn't be an overstatement to call that transformation "pretty extreme." I went from being a reactionary, mentally soft, whiny little twit (okay, let's be honest—I was a BITCH) who was easily thrown off course by even the tiniest problems, to someone who now looks at even the ugliest of situations with a level of confidence I never could have imagined just a few years ago.

I was someone with no emotional regulation who would fly off the handle at the smallest, most ridiculous things. While I'm not going to claim I'm impossible to anger (I'm still human—I have my moments), if someone's goal is to get under my skin, knock me off my game, or fluster me, they're in for a tough time.

But here's where you have an advantage I didn't: I did this by accident. You can approach it with clear intention—something I never knew. However, I believe you have to fully immerse yourself in the principles, pillars, and tactics in this book—leaving no stone unturned. That is, if you want to gain maximum value from it. I also realize that if all of this is new to you, make no mistake, it's a lot easier said than done!

One Final Thought

Now, since you've indulged me by sticking with me through this book, I'll make two offers as I bring this to a close:

First, I'll send you a PDF copy of the "Resilience Regimen Daily Journal" to help you put these principles into practice.

Second, I'll hop on the phone with you for a 15-minute personalized consultation to see how, together, we can make the Resilience Regimen a part of your everyday life.

Just drop me a line at info@marklightgroup, and we'll connect!

No matter where you are in life right now, know this: resilience isn't just something you build—it's something you live. Every step you take, no matter how small, is progress toward becoming the person you're meant to be. So take a deep breath, lean into the discomfort, and remember—you're stronger than you think, and together.........

WE CAN DEAL WITH ANYTHING!

Made in the USA
Columbia, SC
19 February 2025